PERMISSION
to be
POWERFUL

HOW TO STOP PLAYING SMALL, CLAIM YOUR DESIRES AND STEP
INTO THE FULLNESS OF WHO YOU WERE BORN TO BE

ELYSE ARCHER • ASHLEY TAYLOR • LAURA GRABAVOY
ALLISON LACOURSIERE • BROOKE (ANDERSON) LEGGETT
PENNY COOPER • JOHANNA WHITE • DREA BUER
LESLIE THORNTON • JESSICA HERRERA • CHRISTINA VIEIRA

Digital ISBN 979-8-9894972-0-1

Paperback ISBN 979-8-9894972-2-5

Hardcover ISBN 979-8-9894972-3-2

Published by She Sells
ElyseArcher.com

This book is dedicated to you—our reader—and to the transformation that will unfold in your life as you give yourself full permission to be powerful.

Contents

PERMISSION

to be

POWERFUL

HOW TO STOP PLAYING SMALL, CLAIM YOUR DESIRES AND STEP
INTO THE FULLNESS OF WHO YOU WERE BORN TO BE

Introduction

For some of us, it's a moment. A moment where the hair stands up on the back of your neck, and you make the unequivocal declaration that it's time to change. For others, it's a progressive series of choices, each one perhaps seemingly small but add up to a quantum leap looking backward.

Regardless of which path you take, if you're holding this book in your hands, it's likely that you are ready to step into your full power in a greater way. Perhaps that looks like finally leaving the job that pays well but is sucking your soul dry and taking the leap to start your own company. Maybe it's going for the promotion you want at work but don't think you're qualified for. Or on a personal level, it could look like leaving the relationship, giving yourself permission to parent the way you feel called to, or moving cross-country to somewhere you've never been but intuitively feel called to live even though your relatives are telling you you're crazy.

Whatever it is for you, the stories you are about to read in this book are from real women who woke up from the fog we all find ourselves in at some point in our lives and realized that no one was coming to give them permission to be, do, and have what they wanted. That they were the only ones who could give themselves permission to be powerful.

These women are no different from you, with perhaps the exception that they have decided to unapologetically go for what they want (a characteristic I love and admire among the members of our She Sells community).

In fact, the name "She Sells" is deceptive. I started this company in 2020 with the desire to help women master sales, but what the company turned into is so much more. The things that I found truly quantum leaped women's sales were not so much a certain sales strategy, but rather things like:

- Learning how to shift their belief systems to support the bigness of their goals and vision.

- Stepping into higher amounts of worthiness about money, receiving, and visibility.

- Learning how to integrate and blend masculine and feminine energy.

When women mastered these three core areas, their sales skyrocketed as a byproduct of the inner transformation that had occurred. We started to see quantum leaps happening among our community members like:

- Women going from averaging $10K months to making $270K in 90 days.

- Women launching brand-new businesses and being at $50K months within six months.

- Women doubling their income in corporate in a very short time.

And more. You'll hear from some of these women in this book, as well as from others who created their own version of a quantum leap. Their stories will wake you up, inspire you, and hopefully help you take a bold, burn-the-ships type of action toward the thing you know you want to do deep down but have been telling yourself it's not the right time, you're not ready yet, etc.

Here's the truth about quantum leaps—it's never the right time. You'll never see the full path before you start. You'll never have all the resources you need before you begin. But your heart and soul will guide you in the right direction if you're willing to listen.

These women listened, took action, and changed their careers and their lives. Are you ready to do the same? If so—read on, my friend. It's time to trust yourself and your desire for more in your life.

As the great Bob Proctor said, with any goal you are going for, you are trading your life for it. So rather than asking if you are worthy of the goal, you need to ask if the goal is worthy of you.

It's time to set goals worthy of trading your life for.

It's time to give yourself permission to be powerful.

Cheering you on,

Elyse Archer
Founder & CEO, She Sells

Chapter 1

The Fullness of Who You Are

by Elyse Archer

"WHAT HAVE I JUST done?" I asked myself, almost in shock. My heart was racing and my hands were trembling. Thoughts like, *Have I just put my family in financial ruin? Who am I to make this kind of a bold move?* swam around me until I felt like I would drown in them.

Let me back up a few steps and share what happened just a few months prior that led to this moment. On my thirty-fifth birthday, I made a wish that unknowingly would change my life. I remember exactly where I was. I was standing in my three-month-old son's nursery with him and my husband, and we were getting him changed together. The clock struck 5:25 p.m. (my birth time), and I felt compelled to make a wish. (Side note that I trust my fellow parents will appreciate: yes, this life-changing, pivotal moment happened while standing over a dirty diaper pail. The universe does indeed have a sense of humor.)

So anyway, back to the wish. In past years I wished for things like more money or a better home or career. This year, though, something unexpected came to me. I'd been reading *The Top Five Regrets of the Dying* by Bronnie Ware, a hospice worker who sat with hundreds of people at their deathbed and heard their dying wishes. One of the top five that stood out to me was: I wish I'd had the courage to live a life true to myself, not the life others expected of me.

Something about that regret had been eating away at me for the few weeks leading up to my birthday. See, at the time, I was living a life many would call their dream. I was happily married (after having weathered a tough divorce several years prior), had a beautiful three-month-old child, lived in a very nice home, and was a successful entrepreneur doing sales and branding work with some very high-powered clients. On the outside, I seemed to have checked all the boxes for a happy and fulfilled life.

But as I sat late at night reading that book under the glow of a dimly lit lamp while nursing my son, something kept nudging me that part of my life was off track. If I was honest with myself, I had much greater dreams for my life than I was allowing myself to live at that time. I had created a life that was good, but not great.

Deep down I had aspirations to run a company that dramatically impacted the world, make enough money to empower my husband to quit his job and pursue his dream of going to medical school, as well as provide a more expansive lifestyle for my family and make a greater name for myself on the world stage as a thought leader and philanthropist.

For years, I'd been dreaming of doing these things but kept saying "someday" (or as I now call it, "putting my life on layaway"). What I wasn't aware of at the time was that I had given my power away so often earlier in life that I was unconsciously waiting for someone to come tell me I was good enough to do these things, or that it was the right time.

So when the clock struck 5:25 p.m. on my birthday, I made a different kind of wish than I had made on past birthdays. I wished to experience the fullness of who I was. Nothing dramatic happened right at that moment, but what ensued in the following days and months would change the trajectory of my life, and my family's life, forever.

Ask and the Universe Delivers

Have you ever had the experience of asking for something you want and shortly thereafter getting a clear sign from the universe? Very soon after I made that wish and decided I was ready to be done wasting time playing small in my business and life, I heard an ad on a podcast I occasionally listened to from a mentor for moms who want to become millionaires saying that she had a spot open for private coaching. I smiled and said, "All right, universe, I'll bite."

On the discovery call with her, my intuition was scream-
ing at me that I had to say yes to private coaching, and
then I found out the investment—$50K for six months of
private coaching. Even now at the level I've grown to, that
is still a significant investment, but back then it was insane.
I couldn't fathom how I could possibly pay for that and
immediately went into anxiety at the prospect of saying
yes.

My intuition was clearly telling me to move forward,
but my analytical mind was telling me this was crazy—I
didn't even have the money laying around for the $20K
deposit required to get started. Plus, I was the breadwinner
of our family and financially responsible to make sure we
were okay. What if I made a terrible mistake and made our
family destitute?

Your Must Will Move Mountains

Here's the thing about intuition and quantum leaps: what
you are called to do will never make sense on the front
end. It will seem wild, illogical, and unsafe. However, on
the back end, it will make perfect sense. This is, as Steve
Jobs called it, "connecting the dots backward."

Even though I was terrified, I chose to follow my intuition and move forward, putting the deposit on a credit
card. Which brings us back to the moment at the top of
this chapter, where I had just pressed "submit" to pay
the invoice and immediately wondered if I'd just made a

terrible mistake. The power of making a decision though, and what I later learned to understand as "decision-making from the end," is that once you get out of the low-vibe energy suck of "maybe" and just decide, your mind goes to work looking for ways to help you achieve your goal.

It would be fun to say that as soon as I made the decision and decided to quantum leap, huge results started pouring in. However, that's not what happened. I actually went into three weeks of intense self-doubt, facing every money demon I had and wondering if I'd just made a massive mistake. I didn't even know how I was going to pay for the next coaching payments, let alone what I had already put on the credit card.

My coach also had me stepping way out of my comfort zone, doing things like singing publicly on social media (I used to sing but had stopped after being sexually assaulted in college), and launching a new group program even though I had major doubts about whether an entire group of women would want to work with me. *What if no one signs up?* I wondered. But I was committed to doing whatever I was told to do, and I pushed past the fear.

The beautiful thing that happened once I made the commitment to leap and go for what I wanted was that I started serendipitously being connected with resources and opportunities to help me overcome the challenges that previously had kept me stuck. I connected deeply with the work of Bob Proctor and Dr. Joe Dispenza during this time, and even though I had loosely studied them for years, I decided to embody their teachings and really work through any and all limiting beliefs that came up about what I was worthy and capable of.

After three weeks of intensely applying this material, even though nothing had changed yet in my outer world and no additional money had come in, I started to feel different. What I now know, which I didn't then, is that emotion precedes manifestation. Meaning that if you are in a quantum leap, and you have just taken massive action out of faith, as long as you can stay connected to the vision and the emotion of your wish fulfilled, it is literally just a matter of time until that or something better happens. You don't have to be perfect with this; just reconnect with the vision and the emotion of your wish fulfilled as soon as you realize you've fallen off the horse.

As I did this, the consistent, low-grade anxiety that I'd struggled with for years turned into feelings of calm and peace. I started to feel my heart open in ways I hadn't felt my whole adult life, and suddenly I felt so in love with life. I felt like I was in a different realm, and even though fears would still periodically pop up about whether or not I was going to be okay, I knew enough at that point to know that fears and limiting beliefs are lies and was able to quiet them.

(Side note: This is a huge hack for goal achievement. When you are thinking about your goal or taking some action toward it and you feel fear or any lower-level emotion, it literally means in that moment you are thinking a lie;

something that isn't actually true. There is deeper belief rewiring work we do with our clients to help them through this process, but for now, I just want you to have the power of this awareness in your life because it's transformational.)

So fast forward three more weeks, and something crazy happened. As I launched the group program that I thought no one would sign up for, enough new women signed up to have over a $100K launch. Little old me, who had been struggling and stuck at $100K years for over a decade, had just had her first $100K month.

I went on to do over seven figures in sales in the first two years of the brand, and our company continues to prosper and expand today. I have been able to do the things I once only dreamed of like retire my husband from working so he could study for medical school (he is in medical school at the University of New England as I type this), contribute to charities on a much larger scale than I used to, and transform the lives of hundreds of women as a result of our brand. The transformation happened so quickly that it made my head spin. But looking back, I can see that several key things were in place (these are things I love helping my clients implement today):

The Size of the Risk Determines the Size of the Reward

If you aren't willing to "make decisions from the end," meaning make a decision based on what the version of you with your goal achieved would do, you aren't stepping out in enough faith to create a quantum leap. I had heard it said that you should invest 5 to 10 percent of what you want to make into coaching and mentoring, which is how I initially decided it made sense to invest $50K in coaching since I wanted to make $1 million. (I've gone on to invest multiple six figures over the past few years in myself with coaching and mentoring).

However, most people don't operate by this philosophy, and they make decisions based on present facts, like what they have in the bank account or what they've done in the past. Here's the thing—present facts are old news. Start making decisions based on what you want, and you'll attract the ideas, money, and resources to you *after* you have made the decision. If you want a big reward, you are going to have to take big action that probably feels risky to the present version of you. But to the version of you who has your goal accomplished, it makes total sense.

Your Level of Income Will Never Exceed Your Level of Self-Worth

Learning this was huge for me. What prevented me from making more money for a long time, as it does for so many of the clients I now am privileged to serve, was that I actually didn't feel worthy of making more. I had to reprogram and rewire my subconscious mind to feel worthy of the results I wanted. Here's the thing about worthiness when it comes to goals—you are worthy just because you are. In fact, as I stated in the forward, you should stop evaluating whether you are worthy of a certain goal and remember that you trade your life for your goals. As Bob Proctor asked, "Is this goal worthy of trading my life for?"

Your Results Will Never Supersede Your Identity

In the process of my quantum leap, I had to literally become a different person. This is where people get the law of attraction messed up. They think it means that you get what you want. The truth is, you don't get what you want—you get what you *are*.

If you want a different result, start thinking about what a person who has that result would be thinking, feeling, and doing. This is a process in neuroscience called *metacognition*—to think about what you're thinking about. I now have my clients map out their old personality versus the new personality they are stepping into of someone who has their goal achieved, and our work together is in bridging the gap until they literally become the version of them with their goal achieved. From that place, it is literally just a matter of time until it happens.

Your Desires Are Green Lights

One of the most beautiful lessons of giving myself permission to be powerful was learning to trust myself again. After sexual assault and struggling with an eating disorder for over a decade, I had disconnected from my body because my feelings were too painful. Doing the work to get back in touch with my body, and learn to trust its signals again, created a powerful dynamic where I learned to trust my intuition and desires again.

What I now know is that your desires are green lights leading you in the direction of your goals. If I hadn't trusted my desire for more and followed my intuition to invest in a way that most people would have said was crazy, you wouldn't be reading this book today. When you follow your desires, it's not just you who benefits. There are countless others who will win as well; you just won't see it until after you've taken the action.

Think about it:

- When you say yes to investing in coaching or mentorship you feel drawn to, your family and kids benefit from how you transform.

- When you say yes to that dream vacation you want but feel guilty for "splurging" on, you create beautiful memories for yourself and your family for years to come.

- When you go for that raise or promotion at work and you get it, you get to lead and help others in a bigger way in the workplace. *Plus,* you get more money to take care of yourself, and your family, and circulate in the economy.

- When you decide to show up visibly on social media to promote yourself and your business, people who are looking for your product or service actually know you exist (crazy concept, I know) and can hire you to help receive the transformation you provide.

There are countless other examples out there, but the bottom line is that if you trust your calling for more, as I did and each of the women in this book have done, there is a massive blessing for you *and* for others on the other side of it.

When you act in faith on your desires, the money, resources, ideas, and connections you need to fulfill your calling will show up *after* you have made a committed decision and taken action toward your goal. This is both neuroscience and spiritual law.

In your quantum leap journey, you will be required to act in faith and do things that are uncomfortable, but let's be honest—what was once your comfort zone now feels like a cage anyway, doesn't it? You're ready for more. You're ready to expand. But *you* are the only one who can give yourself permission. It's time.

About The Author

Elyse Archer

Elyse Archer is the founder of the Superhuman Selling and She Sells movements, which empower entrepreneurs and sales professionals to revolutionize how they sell, explode their income and achieve quantum leaps in all areas of life.

A 2X Salesforce Top Influencer and a thought leader whose insights have been featured in major media including Forbes and Inc, Elyse is passionate about empowering her clients to sell in a way that leverages their natural gifts, and helps them build wealth along the way. She is an author, an international keynote speaker and host of She Sells Radio, where she shares best practices from female entrepreneurs and sales professionals who have accomplished extraordinary goals.

Connect with Elyse:

Chapter 2

Don't Put Your Life on Layaway

by Ashley Taylor

Lightbulb Moment

SITTING IN THE TERMINAL of the Orange County airport, my mind wandered in anticipation of getting back to my kids after being gone for what felt like an eternity. Fidgeting with my phone, I absentmindedly scrolled through LinkedIn, hoping to pass the time more quickly. Little did I know that a simple phrase would catch me off guard and resonate so deeply within me: "Don't put your life on layaway."

As soon as I read those words, they struck me like a ton of bricks. It was as if the universe had conspired to send me a message at the perfect moment. I paused and allowed the weight of the sentence to sink in.

I'd been gone for a week. Columbus to San Francisco to LA to Columbus. Visiting nine existing and potential clients, engaging in sixteen meetings, and capping each night with events or dinners. Among my colleagues, it had become a running joke: "If you travel with Ashley, be prepared to go nonstop." Secretly, this jest offered a sense of reassurance of my own excuse I'd tell myself about being away—that as long as I was as effective as possible, my absence was justified.

But wow, that phrase "Don't put your life on layaway" spoke to my soul, not only because that's exactly what I had been doing—living in the somedays—but because of how hard I had worked to have this life in the first place.

I had spent years dedicated to building a successful career and, in many ways, had embodied everything I could think of as being a high-achieving professional. The road to this point had been paved with hard work, sacrifices, and a relentless pursuit of excellence. Climbing the corporate ladder, I had become accustomed to the fast-paced rhythm of business trips fueled by the drive to achieve my goals.

Yet, during the constant motion and the pursuit of success, I had unknowingly (okay, maybe even partially knowingly), put my life on layaway. The phrase, though seemingly simple, struck me at my core because it held a mirror up to the reality I had been evading. I had been deferring my dreams, my desires, and presentness with my loved ones to an uncertain future labeled "someday."

As I sat in the airport, a flood of memories washed over me of missed family gatherings, postponed vacations, and delayed moments of joy—all for the sake of professional progress. Each memory carried its weight, compounding the guilt of the choices I had made. *Don't put your life on layaway.* The phrase reverberated in my mind like a mantra, empowering me to confront the conditioning that had held me back. The words were like a wake-up call—an invitation to reassess my priorities and reclaim the power I had unknowingly relinquished. It was not about abandoning my ambitions or forsaking the hard-won successes; rather, it was about embracing the idea that my life, my happiness, and my dreams deserved the same attention and urgency I had devoted to my career.

In that instant, I realized that I held the control to narrate my own life, and it was time to rewrite the script. I committed to being unapologetically authentic and to create space for all aspects of myself—both the career-driven go-getter and the soul yearning for more meaningful connections and experiences.

Shaping the Leap

Let's take a step back . . .

To start, I have a fairly boring backstory to speak of, different from a lot of others that make this kind of leap. I had a wonderful childhood, grew up in a stable upper middle-class family, with no trauma to speak of.

As the oldest of three girls, with relatives highly regarded in the community, there was a sense of responsibility that came with the territory—there were certain expecta-tions. And there was no way myself or my sisters were going to let my family down. So we followed the rules, got good grades, held leadership roles, smiled, and put on the show even when we didn't feel like it. I only slipped up when I felt like I was disappointing others, which led my emotions to pour out of me and was thus dubbed "too emotional." So, of course, as I grew, I conquered how to harness those emotions and push them down—constructing the shield of perfectionism.

Growing up, my perception of money was that fi-nancial security came from putting in long hours and grinding relentlessly to achieve goals. "Money comes from hard work." This ethos was ingrained in me from an early age, shaping my belief that hard work was the key to success. I had an insatiable desire to be successful (whatever that really meant). So the formula seemed quite simple: if I worked hard then I could be in control of my future and so that's exactly what I did. Control brought me comfort—it made me feel calm and safe.

And for most of my life, this formula worked for me. I worked hard to get into the schools I wanted. I set myself up to get every job I ever applied for. And by the time I was twenty-six, I felt established, had married my amazing husband, and I found myself as a senior recruiter at a well-respected automotive engineering services company.

I immediately fell in love with my job. I was captivated by it. The thrill of learning about new technology, the nuances of the product development world, and the sometimes quirky but strong relationships that came with engaging engineers. It was also my perception, however, that because I was in a male-dominated, highly technical industry that I was regarded as "less than." This perception fueled my belief that I had to work twice as hard to earn respect and recognition. I'd relish the moments when I could showcase my in-depth knowledge by grasping complex technical concepts or asking probing questions. I couldn't shake the way others *might* see me—this "little blonde chick," a label I would even give myself in my thoughts. This perception only intensified my drive to work hard and overcome that stigma and prove my worth. So I did.

Over the course of nearly eight years with the company, I embarked on an incredible journey. I started as a recruiter, immersing myself in the world of engineering and automotive, and successfully recruited hundreds of skilled engineers with diverse specialties. As time went on, I set my sights on business development and worked diligently to make my mark in that domain. Eventually, I achieved my goal and headed up all new revenue generation, elevating my role to become one of the top five individuals within our thriving, almost thirty-million-dollar company.

Two things that should be noted when looking back at my tenure at that company: First, the company I worked for was incredible. They trusted me implicitly, and they gave me the room to grow, impact, and make changes. They never pressured—all that, ladies and gents, was self-inflicted. Second, the growth I experienced, of course, didn't happen by accident. I grinded. I worked all hours and prided myself on being the *one* that knew everything going on in the company. The go-to person. "Just ask Ashley, she'll know." I put the success of the company on my own shoulders and carried it as my cross to bear for the good and the bad, almost as a badge of honor. My job became my obsession, and I was a control freak about it.

Detour

Amid the relentless pursuit of control came a detour on my journey—a painful chapter that would forever shape my perception of power and resilience. Like a good little type A planner, I wanted to get pregnant at twenty-seven, just like my mom. Planning down to which month to get pregnant so I could have the baby in just the right month. Because being nine months pregnant in the August heat would be just so damn awful.

With every negative pregnancy test, control slipped through my fingers. My carefully constructed facade of control was now orchestrated by two-week waits, hormone levels, ultrasounds, and procedures. As I faced the heart-wrenching reality of infertility, I was told that IVF was my best option. But still, I was determined that with hard work this, too, was something I could control. So I did all the things: adjusted my diet, took the medications, timed "things" correctly. And it landed me one ectopic pregnancy, but nothing else.

After twelve rounds of treatments including Clomid, Femara, IUIs, and hormone shots, life had cunningly stolen my power, leaving me in a state of limbo and vulnerability. I eventually surrendered and came to terms that it was finally time for IVF.

Our IVF processes surpassed expectations, resulting in fifteen surviving embryos, of which eight were genetically tested and found to be perfectly normal—a feat even my renowned doctor had never witnessed before. Miraculously, we found ourselves pregnant with a baby boy. Needless to say, we were overjoyed. Over the following weeks, we saw him grow from a blob to a gummy bear, heard his heartbeat, and when it came time for our last appointment to "graduate" from our fertility doctor and get released to our OB, we were ecstatic.

You know where this is going, so I'm going to spare myself the pain of all the detail. But four little words, "There is no heartbeat," sent me spiraling into depression and deep, overall rage. Rage at my body, rage at God and the universe, rage at others who were able to get pregnant so easily.

The harrowing emotions of grief, anger, and fear blurred the lines between my corporate success and personal fulfillment. I clung to my corporate addiction even tighter. My job became a refuge, a realm where I could still grasp some semblance of control and validation. I pushed myself beyond limits, believing that by proving my indispensability to the company, I could fill the void left by the absence of a child. Proving to myself that I was still enough.

We charged onward and after three years of treatments, loss, and an insurmountable amount of tears via IVF, we finally had our long-awaited son. Twenty months later, we had our daughter. It's unimaginable to think that if we hadn't experienced the struggle and the loss at that time that our two perfect little ones might not be in our lives. Of course, that's easier to say in retrospect.

Here's where you were probably expecting the epiphany moment because I finally got the blessings I had wanted for so long. I finally got my life back and the wake-up call for my priorities to shift. But it wasn't.

I remember detailing out my maternity leave plans like they were a war tactic. Every what-if accounted for. Every single task was added in people's calendars ahead of time and even scheduled emails were sent "from me" while I was out to remind people of projects and things that they needed to be thinking about. All while in the background checking every email that I demanded being copied on, texting people so HR wouldn't find out, and doing research and reading about the latest trends in the industry so I wasn't behind. Both maternity leaves, I ended up coming back early because I felt like the company "needed me." In some ways I guess it's nice to feel needed, but really, looking back, I think it stemmed from insecurity that I'd lose the respect and control that I had worked so hard for.

As this new era of being a mom unfolded, thoughts of inadequacy, guilt, and judgment constantly filled my head. I loved my little ones so much but self-doubt, anxiety, and comparison consumed me. Again, in seeking the feeling of control, I found refuge at work. Where I could feel like a badass—confident, strong, sure of myself. Where I could see that I was making an impact—bringing in millions of dollars in revenue and some huge-name clients. Where I could get the quick satisfaction of seeing my fingerprints by negotiating contracts, developing our value prop, formulating company strategy. I was addicted to the influence, the approval, the respect, the control. It was exhilarating. It was exhausting.

Burnout

Truthfully, I actually didn't even realize that I was burned out. I didn't realize how much I had my head down, charging ahead, and was never coming up for air. And then, there I was, sitting in that airport scrolling through LinkedIn and got slapped in the face. I don't know why it was that moment. I don't know why it was that specific phrase, at that particular time, but it just all came flooding to me. I was building a company for somebody else; I was living my life for the future and not living my life for the right now. I was missing my kids' toddler years, and I was never going to get those back. I was not being fully present for these two little humans that I had worked so incredibly hard to have in the first place.

For the next few months following that trip, I tried to tell myself it was just a phase. That the yearning feeling would go away. That it was just part of the ebb and flow of working and the sales cycle. When I'd get too far down the path of wanting more, I'd bring myself back with thinking things like "How could the company survive without me?" "What will they do?" "It's not fair and will put too much pressure on the remaining team." I told myself that I was being selfish. Could I never just be happy? How could I want more when I had so much? I'm just being too emotional.

On the outside, my life was pretty darn perfect. A wonderful family with a supportive husband and adorable, well-behaved kids. A beautiful house in a neighborhood full of our friends and other children. Health. And a stable job that I had busted my butt to work my way up to and was now respected, influential, and making a sizable six-plus-figure income. I had gotten exceptional at putting on the costume of having it all together, I had lost sight of the joy that once fueled my ambitions, and my days blurred into a monotonous routine of chasing success without truly living. But I knew deep down that something was off. There had to be a reason I couldn't get the feeling of wanting more out of my head.

We took a long vacation to Disney, thinking that would satiate my need for my time with family and rid the burnout that I was feeling. Instead, it just opened my eyes even more to the reality that I was done with this part of my life. That anything I had built, any respect or approval I had gotten, impact made, just was not worth it. And I knew that deep down I had to let go of the control that I had spent so many years trying to develop. It no longer served me.

Beginning to Give Permission

With that, I took my first step into uncharted territory—the realm of self-discovery and permission to dream. What truly mattered to me? What ignited the fire within my soul? It was time to envision a life where I was present, truly living it, and doing exactly what I wanted.

I decided to embark on a thought experiment: What if money wasn't a factor and success was guaranteed? It was a question my husband and dad had asked me for years—encouraging me to open my own company. Until now, I had brushed it off, deeming it "not the right time" or dismissing it as lacking the perfect concept.

But as I relinquished the reins of control, ideas flooded my mind. Pieces of my passions started to fit together like a puzzle. I discovered that engaging with people, facilitating connections, and problem-solving fueled me. The intricacies of technology intrigued the nerd within me—I loved understanding how and why things worked, connecting the dots like a master puzzle solver. And then there was my fascination with sustainability—the constant advancements, the impact on the world around us, and the passionate pursuit of betterment for the sake of my children's future.

Individually, these passions lit me up, but now I saw the threads intertwining, forming a picture of what my life could be. In continuation of letting go and dreaming, within two days I heard this term "green technology" and the lightbulb moment occurred. Leveraging my vast network and extensive industry knowledge, I could help growing green tech organizations to scale their workforce and ultimately save them time. And GreenTech Resources was born—a recruiting company focusing on connecting exceptional people with innovative organizations.

As the weeks passed, my conviction and confidence only grew stronger. I made the decision, and with a sense of nervous pride, I gave my notice to the company that had been a comfort zone for so long. Leaving the security of my stable job behind wasn't an act of recklessness—it was a leap of faith, fueled by the clarity I had found.

In giving myself the permission I needed to let go, I realized that I no longer craved external validation. The desire to please had been rooted in the little girl within me, yearning for approval and respect from others. But now, I had come to understand that the only validation that truly mattered was my own—the validation that came from living life authentically, without apology or reservation.

So Here I Am . . .

So here I am, embracing the freedom to pave my own path—one step at a time. This journey of self-discovery is fueled by the audacity to dream and the courage to chase my passions. That little girl inside me has grown wiser, understanding that life's value isn't determined by others' opinions. It's about owning my power, relishing every moment, and finding fulfillment in my authentic self.

As I write this chapter, five months into leaving my corporate job and taking the leap, I can't help but feel a sense of immense excitement and fulfillment. There's no turning back now, and I wouldn't have it any other way. The veil has been lifted, and for the first time, I can truly see the magnificent possibilities ahead. And once you feel it, once you see it, you can't put the toothpaste back into that tube. Each morning brings excitement and clarity as I embark on this adventure of living life my way. I mean, who wouldn't want to live life on their own terms?

You might say, "She's just in the honeymoon phase, there's no guarantee her company is going to work out." Sure, maybe not forever. But what guarantees in life do you really have? And are there going to be hardships and bumps and bruises along the way? Absofreakinlutely. But one thing I know for certain is that I will be present to enjoy that journey, and if it's not this, I know in my soul it's something better.

Takeaways

I'm not saying go quit your job tomorrow like I did; every-one has their own path. But I am saying take some time to reflect. Are you actually living your life or are you going through the motions? If there were no consequences, what would you be doing right now? Start with little things and build from there.

And to be clear, I'm not perfect. I don't have this all figured out, and this mindset shift is something I'm con-tinually working on each and every day. But I know I'm on the right track. My heart swells with pride and boundless gratitude when I reflect on the leap I took—to grant myself permission to be present, to embrace life, and to never put it on layaway again.

About The Author

Ashley Taylor

With 13+ years in recruitment and engineering sales, Ashley Taylor is a guiding light in the energy, transportation, and mobility sectors. Her insights into workforce development stem from thousands of interactions with engineers & operations professionals, from legacy brands like Honda to startups like Rivian.

Ashley is celebrated for her knack for forming swift, strong connections. Her authenticity and deep empathy enable her to bridge gaps between organizations and talent. These relational skills, combined with her out-of-the-box thinking, are key to her success. Motivated by her commitment to making a difference, Ashley found-ed Green Tech Resources and ChargedUp Careers, symbolizing her dedication to pairing innovative organizations with top talent. With her passion for career alignment and deep expertise, she ensures professionals find roles where they genuinely flourish.

Outside work, Ashley cherishes moments with her family. Whether it's basking by Lake Erie or venturing on family escapades with her husband, Austin, and children, Beckett and Piper, she deeply values meaningful connections.

Ashley wholeheartedly believes in living by the golden rule and that a smile is contagious, showcasing her unwavering optimism. This blend of expertise and heartfelt values makes Ashley a standout in her domain.

Connect with Ashley:

Chapter 3

Permission to Heal

by Laura Grabavoy

HOW DO YOU FEEL better when you feel so much pain and hurt by others?

My fortyish-year-old self sat on the couch with a bottle of cabernet, winding down from a long day. It had been another in a string of days from hell filled with work issues, distractions, and frustration. The way other people monopolized my calendar, their emergencies becoming mine, left me with barely enough time to grab lunch or take a bathroom break and had long since become the norm in my life.

This particular day had been a doozy. It started when I woke up late (again) and couldn't fit in a workout before heading to work. Then, I went out of my way to introduce my partners to a new potential client, and they reciprocated by excluding me from an important meeting. Later, my workday was interrupted when one of my kids was late for school (again) and needed me to call in an excuse. The interruptions continued, this time to transfer money into a school account so my other child could buy lunch. Why couldn't I get a break? By the time I got home, I was beyond annoyed and way too exhausted to fit in an evening workout.

Then I realized I forgot to take anything out for dinner and ended up ordering pizza (again), which left me feeling guilty and only fueled the building resentment. Why was I the one who always had to deal with everything kid and meal-related? Pissed off at my husband, frustrated by my kids, and drained by life, I was totally depleted and had nothing left to give to anyone. Hence the bottle of cabernet.

As I was scrolling through social media to check out from the chaos of the day, this live IG series popped up from Elyse Archer. I had been following her for a while and remembered she was doing a series based on the book *Ask and It Is Given* by Esther and Jerry Hicks called "Releasing Resistance to What You Want." I tuned in and the next thing I know I am putting a comment in to ask a question for live coaching: *How can I feel better when I feel so hurt by others?*

As soon as I realized what I'd done, I looked for a way to undo it. Was there a way to retract my question? I looked around the screen frantically while all the doubts ran through my head:

What a stupid question.

People are going to judge me.

Who is this Elyse woman, anyway?

She isn't going to be able to help.

She doesn't know me or anything about me.

She doesn't know I had been married for twenty-seven years to my high school sweetheart. She doesn't know we got married at eighteen because we were pregnant with our first son. She doesn't know about the hardship of my past or the trauma of being sexually abused by my stepfather as a child. She doesn't know I have been on my own since I was sixteen years old. She doesn't know anything about my narcissistic mother or dysfunctional family. She doesn't know how much work it took to have the life I have today and what I have built. How is she *really* going to help me? I was so stupid for doing this.

And then it was my turn. Elyse read my question: "How can I feel better when I feel so hurt by others?" I felt like I was going to throw up. And then the next words she spoke sent me into a tailspin: "You have to stop looking outside yourself for how you feel."

I was so confused. Why wouldn't I look outside? I felt the way I did because of the way other people were hurting me, because of the way they took from me without giving anything back. I didn't choose to feel this way.

While I was still trying to understand the first statement, Elyse continued, "You have control over your internal thoughts and emotions."

Then she led me through an exercise. She explained that I could choose to feel better simply by placing my attention on a better feeling. She told me to think of a thought that brought me joy. I instantly thought of my kids and how I love being their mother. She asked if I could feel how this made me feel in my body. I could feel this love in my heart and body. And I felt . . . better.

But Elyse wasn't finished. She continued, "Your outer world is a reflection of you."

I felt like she'd slapped me in the face. Was she telling me it was my fault? That I was the one creating all the negativity I felt in my life? What the hell? I have done everything in my power to make others happy. It's not my fault I was sexually abused. It's not my fault my husband is being a jerk, my kids are ungrateful, and the people at work are selfish and lazy.

Then she said, "Go within to feel better."

What does that even mean? How do I go within? How I was feeling wasn't my fault. It was everyone and everything around me causing my pain. I wanted them to take responsibility for what they did to me. If they changed, it would make things better and I could feel better.

These were things done to me. I didn't choose these things in my life. I spent most of my life trying to be a good person and doing what I could to make my life better. I didn't understand what was wrong with me and why others didn't give a sh*t about my needs or feelings. Why were these things happening to me? Why did life and everyone in my life feel like they were against me?

I watched the recording over and over. She had stirred something inside of me that sparked my inner knowing.

Some part of me knew she was right, even if I didn't fully understand it. Another part of me resisted the idea that I was somehow responsible for feeling so terrible all the time. I spent weeks steeped in this inner turmoil and came out on the other side filled with uncertainty but committed to the journey.

Tools for the Journey Within

In my journey of self-discovery, I realized that going within meant attentively observing my thoughts, actions, and emotions. Instead of blaming others, I started taking responsibility for my feelings. My tendency to prioritize others' happiness over my own led to feelings of hurt and exhaustion. I had linked my self-worth to pleasing others and relied on their responses to validate myself. If things were peaceful and good, I was peaceful and good. If someone was upset, I would try and figure out how to make them happy. I worked hard at earning their love and being enough for them. When I felt like I failed at this, I would beat myself up and feel hurt, blame them or myself, and pull away. When I was seeking validations from others, I found myself feeling guilty, not enough, and hurt, and I would try to fix things. I needed them to change to feel better.

I recognized that I was giving away my power by constantly seeking approval. Taking my power back involved acknowledging that my self-worth wasn't tied to others' opinions of me. I learned that their reactions were beyond my control, and I shouldn't shoulder the responsibility for their feelings. By reframing my mindset, I stopped being a victim and relying on others to change for my well-being.

I created purposeful rituals that became my compass for introspection and were empowering tools for my journey within. Among these, I carved out dedicated time and a sanctuary for myself; it was a refuge where self-discovery could come naturally. The practice of meditation had a pivotal role in silencing external noise and allowing me to attune to my inner voice. Through reading, I discovered perspectives that enriched my own understanding. Journaling was a means to sift through my thoughts, unravel emotions, and change my mindset.

These rituals were the cornerstone for my transformation and diving deeper into my self-exploration of going within.

Create Time and Space

I consciously carved out dedicated time and established a personal sanctuary each morning, gradually incorporating various self-connecting rituals throughout my day. This commitment to creating time and space for myself was important to me, as it became the cornerstone for my inner peace and daily preparation. I recognized that the path to self-discovery required my dedicated effort, prompting me to make the conscious decision to embark on this transformative journey.

This self-preservation initiative stemmed from the realization that my daily routine left me feeling drained, as I often woke up to attend to everyone else's needs first before my own. Initially, I allocated a half hour to this practice, but as time went on, I craved more, thereby allowing me to expand and prioritize self-care in my life.

Throughout this process, I emphasized patience and self-kindness. It was not an act of self-punishment or perfection, but rather a journey of self-discovery and self-nurturing. This shift in mindset required me to affirm my self-worth and acknowledge that I deserved the time for my well-being. As I began to feel better and more energized, I embraced each day with renewed strength, ready to give my best.

I often repeated the affirmation "I deserve this time for myself because I am worth it and can give my best."

Of course, this transformation was not without its challenges. My established routine and the expectations of those around me made it difficult to enact this new ritual. I communicated my needs to my family, adjusted my evening routine to prepare for the mornings, and adjusted my schedule by getting up earlier and going to bed earlier as well.

I remember struggling with guilt when I started this ritual in the morning. I questioned if it was worth it, as I felt I could gain a head start on my day by attending to my to-do list. I worried that I might be neglecting my responsibilities to my husband, children, and dog. Nevertheless, I soon discovered that dedicating time to self-care allowed me to focus more efficiently and accomplish tasks with more energy, inner peace, and clarity. When I neglected this crucial time, I noticed increased scatterbrain tendencies, negative emotions, and a greater sense of depletion. I reassured myself that by prioritizing self-care, I was ultimately benefiting not only myself but also my children, husband, and dog by becoming more peaceful, energized, and centered.

Reading/Meditation

The practice of meditation had a pivotal role in silencing external noise and allowing me to attune to my inner voice. Through reading, I discovered perspectives that enriched my own understanding. Reading has helped me see the world differently. I've read many books that have been a big part of my journey for healing. Two of them are by Dr. Joe Dispenza: *Breaking the Habit of Being Yourself* and *Becoming Supernatural.* These books have been instrumental in reshaping my life, helping me embrace meditation and confront the conditioned emotions that stemmed from my past experiences of victimhood. They were a guiding light in helping me embrace meditation and weaving it into my morning ritual.

Meditation played a huge role in calming my mind and helping me connect with my inner self. I owe my introduction to Dr. Joe Dispenza's work to Elyse, whose guidance proved invaluable. Dr. Joe's teachings shed light on the intricate connection between our thoughts, actions, and emotions in shaping our personalities. Prior to this awakening, I found myself trapped in a constant state of survival, haunted by the memories of past pain and victimhood.

Haunted by the memories of sexual abuse and domestic violence had etched feelings of guilt, shame, powerlessness, and unworthiness deep within my psyche. My entire identity seemed to have been constructed around these painful experiences, and I couldn't seem to escape the painful grip it had on me. Every time I revisited or shared them with others, it felt like I was reliving those painful experiences. I identified myself as a victim and kept repeating the same patterns, like not trusting myself or others, and it felt like an endless cycle.

But then I integrated Dr. Joe Dispenza's guided meditations and teachings from his books into my morning ritual. Initially, I was skeptical of the meditations, but the practice soon became something I looked forward to. I felt strange at first, as if I stumbled upon something mystical or unconventional. However, the transformation I experienced was undeniable.

With consistent practice and a resolution to reshape my identity, coupled with the infusion of positive emotions, I began to liberate myself from the memories of my past. Meditation became a gateway to my future, a future freeing me from the pain and constraints of my past self. It was a journey from reliving my past to forging a new future.

Journaling

Journaling became another powerful tool in my journey of self-discovery. It was a means to shift through my thoughts, unravel emotions, and change my inner mindset. Initially, it wasn't easy. Fear gripped me as I contemplated putting my true feelings on paper. But I reminded myself that it was a safe space to express my thoughts and emotions.

Gratitude lists were a starting point for my journaling sessions. I was used to waking up and thinking about my problems and complaining about my responsibilities for the day. My intention was to change this pattern and start my day with gratitude. I once heard that if we woke up with only what is on our gratitude list, we'd be more mindful of what truly matters. So I began my journey with gratitude. I also delved into my energy levels, noting what energized me and what drained me throughout the day. This gave me insight into what I wanted to change and do differently the next day.

Furthermore, journaling became a refuge to process complex emotions, especially when I felt angry or triggered by my interactions with others. Expressing my anger had always been a challenge for me, but through journaling, I found a way to navigate and process these emotions. It revealed limiting beliefs that held me back, allowing me to rework them into affirmations that would reshape my thoughts.

For instance, I realized that my innate desire to comfort and help others also led me to seek their approval constantly. I shifted my affirmations to focus on self-approval and valuing my own opinion. "I approve of myself" and "My opinion matters" became my daily mantras.

Creating time and space for meditation, journaling, reading, and self-reflection were immediate steps I took to go within, and they brought about noticeable improvements in a short time frame. Showing up for myself and dedicating time to self-growth allowed me to experience profound shifts and transformations in my life.

These changes, however, were not instant gratifications; they required intention and commitment. As I continued to love and invest in myself, I witnessed the remarkable transformations that unfolded when I gave myself permission to explore the depths of my inner world and go within.

Giving Myself Permission

Permission to Trust and Approve Myself
Trusting and approving myself were big shifts I experienced. Being a victim of sexual abuse taught me to not trust myself and to doubt myself. I felt like life and everyone was against me and had a guard up. My self-esteem was low, and I needed others to affirm what I was doing to feel

accepted. I didn't want to cause waves with anyone. I relied on others' opinions to feel safe and secure in my choices. I learned my self-esteem was tied to my self-worth, and I tried to earn the approval of others to feel worthy. I learned how to feel safe in my body again by affirming I had all the answers inside, and I could trust myself. I had to remind myself I was no longer a victim of my past sexual abuse. I started affirming how life was for me, and I started looking for the highest and good in all people.

I experienced the biggest shift with my husband when I approved and trusted myself in our relationship. I was the only one who could approve and trust myself, and he couldn't do this for me. When I looked for him to do this for me, it pushed him away because of my insecurity. I was constantly looking for him to affirm his love for me. I stopped doing this and started to look for the good in him and what I loved. I stopped criticizing him as a way to fix and control him. It helped us to create more love and joy in our relationship.

Permission to Heal and Not Get Over Myself

I used to believe that I needed to "get over myself" or "get over a situation." These self-limiting beliefs often surfaced when I confronted triggers stemming from my traumatic experiences of sexual abuse and my complex relationship with my mother. These phrases had become deeply ingrained in my mind, and I caught myself repeating them whenever I faced particularly challenging situations.

However, I gradually came to realize that this belief system was undermining my self-worth. It was as if it told me that I wasn't deserving of the time and effort it takes to heal. These thoughts left me feeling small and unworthy. I eventually came to a profound realization: I didn't have to "get over" these intensely painful emotions, and they certainly wouldn't disappear. Instead, I needed to give myself permission to heal from them, to acknowledge and address the pain without trying to dismiss or ignore it.

In this process, I discovered that I held the power to slow things down for myself. I could make the conscious decision that I was worth the time and effort required for healing.

Permission to Forgive Myself and Others

My perspective had a profound transformation upon encountering a simple yet powerful phrase: "People can only love others to the capacity that they love themselves, and I could only love others to the capacity that I loved myself." This revelation shifted my understanding of human behavior. I realized that the actions and emotions of others were not a reflection of my worth but rather a manifestation of their own true self-love or lack thereof. It became clear that without self-love and inner work, I couldn't give love to myself or anyone else.

Forgiveness took on a new meaning for me. It ceased to be solely about absolving those who hurt me; instead, it became a vital act of self-compassion. It was about allowing myself to navigate through my unsettled, deep array of emotions—hate, anger, sadness, and hurt—and ultimately releasing them. I recognized that those who had wronged me needed to enter their journey of self-forgiveness. Forgiveness, I learned, was a practice of reconciliation of oneself.

One of my favorite forgiveness exercises, Ho'oponopono, is a Hawaiian tradition consisting of four powerful but simple phrases:

I am sorry.

Please forgive me.

Thank you.

I love you.

Whenever I felt wounded, angry, or triggered by past events or memories, I turned to these words. The simplicity of the words were matched only by the immense emotional release they triggered. I discovered that loving oneself is the best elixir for healing. As I embarked on my own healing journey, I witnessed a ripple effect that extended to those around me.

Forgiving others did not necessarily mean having them in my life. I realized I had the ability to choose who belonged in my inner circle and who did not. Some relationships evolved positively as a result, while others needed to be released to facilitate my personal growth and well-being.

Healing got easier when I focused on it being a part of my journey and not a destination. I had been so determined to just get over my pain, but that isn't the same as healing. I shifted my focus on enjoying life, being present and accepting that healing is a part of the journey. My pain had a story it was trying to tell me. It held beliefs that were both helpful and limiting. I put healing down when it became heavy. I didn't want to keep living in the stories of my past and reliving the pain to try and force the healing. I focused on creating the life I wanted. I allowed myself to face the pain and release it, and the more I did it, the easier it got. This has brought me so much peace and healing.

I share my story and journey to show you we all have a choice and the power to heal ourselves. We deserve inner peace, and we don't need to wait for anyone or anything outside ourselves to change so we can feel peaceful. My hope is that my story inspires you to go within, heal, and create a new version of the person you want to be. The permission is yours if *you* choose.

About The Author

Laura Grabavoy

Laura is a seasoned professional with over three decades of experience in corporate sales, where she has consistently demonstrated excellence and leadership. As a Vice President, Sales Manager, and Vice President Senior Private Banker, she has built a distinguished career, working with Ultra High Net Worth Clients and leading her teams to remarkable success. Laura's ability to connect with clients and understand their unique needs has earned her several top sales awards and the respect of her peers in the industry.

Laura's expertise extends beyond sales; she is an adept leader in client acquisition and growth, highlighted by her top revenue growth award in the Chicago market and her national ranking. Her career has been marked by a series of notable achievements, including the 2022 Legends Winner Award, recognizing her as a top 1% sales achiever bank-wide.

Laura's professional success is paralleled by her profound personal transformation. Overcoming childhood trauma and a pervasive sense of deep dissatisfaction, she embarked on a healing journey that reshaped her life. Learning to thrive despite external challenges, Laura unlocked new levels of growth, both personally and professionally. This profound personal evolution ignited her passion for helping others, particularly accomplished yet emotionally drained women.

Now, Laura dedicates herself to guiding women through deep emotional healing and self-awareness. She empowers them to reconnect with their higher selves, healing trauma and overcoming everyday stress, self-neglect, and self-doubt. Her approach is not just about achieving professional success but fostering a state of empowerment and self-love, enabling women to live fully, embracing both their professional ambitions and personal desires.

Connect with Laura:

Chapter 4

Pinch Me Moments

by Allison Lacoursiere

MY MOM HAS AN expression she uses for those moments when life feels perfectly gorgeous, and you can't quite believe you're living in that very moment—the ones that leave you breathless, your heart so full it feels like it might burst, your eyes on the verge of happy tears, and you are so present that time seems to stand still. My mom would always say, "Pinch me," as if by pinching ourselves we could awaken from this enchanting dream.

Throughout my life, I've experienced many of these "pinch me" moments. They were so surreal and extraordinary that my eyes struggled to comprehend what they were seeing. It felt incredible to be the one experiencing such beauty and magic. During these moments, I would almost detach from my body, observing the scene and myself within it, overwhelmed with gratitude and love. These moments came to me frequently.

I was born a dreamer, a free spirit, an adventurous soul. My wandering and fearless nature took me on incredible journeys and adventures across the world. It led a small-town Canadian girl like me to build a life on a stunning island, establish a successful business and career as a professional coach, travel extensively, find a partner who shared my passion, and create a beautiful home with him.

For many years, I firmly believed in my power and responsibility to shape my own life. I felt an urgency to avoid stagnation and resist an ordinary life. This motivated me to work hard, stay disciplined, and push myself to achieve my goals. I knew that I possessed the ability to dream, visualize, and bring my ideal life into existence. I lived with the conviction that anything I wished to create was possible, and I could design the most extraordinary life for myself. Those who knew me well were drawn to my optimism, openheartedness, compassion, and love for life. I started helping other women create and design their most meaningful and aligned lives.

However, everything came to a startling halt with one "pinch me" moment. It was the first time I watched myself experience such a moment, but the woman within it seemed unfamiliar. I felt scared for her. I didn't know her.

In that moment that changed my entire life, I could sense the pain, fear, panic, and deep, raw, overwhelming sadness seeping into the depths of my heart. I could feel it all. Yet, it didn't seem possible that these events were happening to me. Not the woman who created an identity based on living a purposeful and meaningful life. Not the young, passionate woman who was so full of life, love, and optimism.

As I sat in my body, gazing at my injured feet, feeling physical pain and my trembling hands, with the police officer opening the car door, my dog pressed against me, shaking, and my car filled with the disarrayed remnants of my former home, I found myself in a state of shock, looking back at the officer.

"Are you okay?" he asked.

"Am I okay?" I couldn't even begin to answer that question. At that moment, I didn't know if I would ever be okay again.

I couldn't recognize the woman I had become. I wished I could just pinch myself and make it all disappear.

I distinctly remember two thoughts that crossed my mind: *I'm so grateful we don't have a child* and *How did I end up here?*

That one "pinch me" moment shattered my heart and more intensely, my inner trust.

The sight of a broken and wounded woman fleeing her home and husband did not align with the vision I had created for myself. It wasn't the life I had worked so tirelessly to build. I couldn't recognize this woman who lacked safety, power, and was now running for help. I didn't know who she was.

After an experience like this, I couldn't return to my old life. It no longer existed in the way I had envisioned and constructed it. It was not safe. I knew that I couldn't go back after this. This was too far, too much.

It wasn't the specific moment that caused my heart to break; rather, it was the realization that I had built my life on an unstable foundation. Deep down, I knew that a man should never inflict physical harm on a woman, especially not the man she loves. But there was a part of me that realized this was partly a result of my own choices. I didn't envision it for myself specifically, but I didn't make the decisions, set the boundaries, or walk away to value myself more than the way I had been living for the past few years.

Abuse like this does not happen in a week or in a day. For me, it was a slow burn. The lies, manipulation, and scary moments started small and gained momentum as the stakes got higher and the walls to escape became harder.

The "pinch me" moment was simply so dramatic that I couldn't ignore the fact that I had built my entire life on a shaky foundation. The hardest part to resolve in my own mind was that if you had asked me if I knew that I was building on a shaky foundation, the answer would have been yes. I knew all along. I could feel it. I could see the signs. I could feel that things were not right. It took me being physically harmed, needing to escape, and feeling broken to be able to walk away and admit that it was not the beautiful life that I had created.

I had let the vision for my future, my goals, and my striving to build the life I was dreaming of become more important and take priority over my own intuition, knowing, and ultimately my safety.

The weeks after the "pinch me" moment were filled with deep shame, fear, anxiety, sadness, and more pain than I knew I could handle. I walked away from my life and my husband completely and focused on regaining my footing, but mostly trying to answer the question: *Why?*

What caused my dreaming, fearless heart to allow this experience into my life? Why didn't I walk away sooner? Why would I allow someone to treat me like that? How could I marry someone like that? The questions were incessant. I blamed myself. I felt insecure, embarrassed, and ashamed.

The one thing that I did know was that the only way and the only one to start building a foundation for my life that would bring me real joy, beauty, peace, and safety was me. I knew that I needed to understand all of the programming and beliefs about myself that would allow me to choose a partner who would physically harm me and lie to me so badly.

The months after were consumed by self-understanding, reflection, coaching, therapy, and healing. I journaled, read, took online courses, looked at my family history, and finally found the answer I was looking for.

Worthiness.

Our self-worth guides all of our decisions in our subconscious mind. It determines what we say yes to and what we will say no to. How much we value ourselves determines how well we take care of ourselves and what we allow into our lives. It is the little moments that shape the big ones.

I was determined to foster and develop my own self-worth, and after a year of research and writing, I found these four steps to be the way to build a life with a foundation that will help you create a life of your wildest dreams, full of "pinch me" moments, and will never lead you to harm and abuse. Here are my four steps to worthiness:

Know Yourself

We often hide from the parts of ourselves that we are scared to face. Worthiness requires you to step into your shadow corners that you tend to avoid. It means embracing memories of your younger self, your family, and anything you feel ashamed of, and remembering who you really are and where you came from. The first step to worthiness is to get to know yourself and see all aspects of the whole person you are.

Accept Yourself

After getting to know who you really are, you may discover things you don't like or wish were different. You might feel ashamed of where you came from or what has happened to you. Truly accepting yourself means seeing yourself exactly as you are, without wanting to change anything about you in that moment. Acceptance doesn't mean you don't want to grow and evolve; it means accepting the person you are and seeing yourself as worthy.

Honor Yourself

As you know who you are and have accepted exactly who you are, you will notice that you can see and hear what you need more clearly. You will have a better connection to your gut, your intuition, your inner knowing. The choice to honor that voice and knowing will lead you to difficult conversations and decisions, but ultimately, it will create the worthiness to put yourself first and take excellent care of yourself. You will make choices that honor the being that you are, with all your uniqueness, desires, dreams, and needs. This is foundational for living a life of true alignment, where you prioritize yourself over the expectations and pressures of the world.

Love Yourself

The final step that naturally follows the first three steps is to truly love who you are. It is to feel joy with your own being, your own self. It's to feel inner peace, joy, and connection to the most amazing parts of you. Life gets to be easy, safe, and peaceful because you know that as you are, you are worthy of goodness, love, and connection. You inherently feel worthy of being treated with respect and love because you are a valuable person without needing to prove yourself, compete, or earn your worth. You are worthy just because you are you, and you have always been and will always be that way.

You have the power to foster and develop the highest level of worthiness. Living a life feeling worthy will carry you into the most aligned, beautiful, and authentic life you could ever imagine. It will create a deep power inside of you that no one will ever be able to take away. You will be your own greatest advocate, keep yourself safe, and take amazing care of the incredible soul that you are. If you have lived a life that has not honored your own worthiness, it's okay. There is always time to create a new life, there is always time to start again. Release your shame, guilt, and fear. It is time to step into your worthiness and choose the life that you are meant for.

And remember, you are worthy just as you are.

About The Author

Allison Lacoursiere

Allison Lacoursiere, the creator of the Clear Aligner Systemization methodology and founder of Clear Coaching, is a leading expert in Clear Aligner Operations. With over a decade of dental experience and multiple certifications, including Registered Dental Assistant and Orthodontic Assistant, Allison collaborates with dental practices to optimize efficiency and boost productivity.

She is a respected faculty member of Align Technology, Upgrade Dental, and the Dental Speakers Institute. Allison's passion for coaching and consulting extends to helping dental offices enhance their culture and revenue by streamlining operations and improving team dynamics. Her expertise also spans the realm of social media marketing as the co-founder of Clearly.IG, where she not only manages social accounts but coaches teams on successful marketing strategies.

Allison hosts 'The Clear Perspective' podcast, featuring industry leaders discussing various dental topics. In addition to her professional achievements, she's a member of the Bermuda National Beach Volleyball Team and a certified personal trainer and yoga instructor. Allison is dedicated to helping individuals and practices achieve their full potential and growth.

Connect with Allison:

Chapter 5

The Power of Yes

by Brooke (Anderson) Leggett

HAVE YOU EVER BEEN working somewhere or working for someone and you just know it isn't right for you? Where every day seems to become increasingly more frustrating and unfulfilling in a job you once loved? It becomes harder to show up completely, and the only things that really keep you going in those moments are the connections you make with the people you interact with on a day-to-day basis.

I was in that situation the first time I said yes to myself in a powerful way. I was working for a real estate investment firm and recently moved from Ohio to Colorado to help open a new market. I had been with this company for about three years at this point and was hell-bent on making partner. But after a few months in Colorado, my heart was telling me something different.

I've always enjoyed learning about people, hearing their stories, and learning what things they are passionate about. To double down, I especially love hearing and learning about the things people are passionate about. The process of helping someone find the right apartment gave me plenty of opportunity to ask the right questions and get to know the people I was helping. I am a true believer that you never know who you are talking to, how you can impact that person's life positively, and how they might impact yours. So be kind and curious. Ask the questions and dig in when you find what they are passionate about, what makes them light up.

I was helping a woman and her girlfriend move into their first apartment together. I went through my usual round of questions: "What size apartment are you looking for? When do you want to move in? What are the top three things your apartment must have?" and found a unit that fit their needs and off we went to check it out. I noticed that this woman was dressed to a T in professional business attire. I started to ask about what she did for work, which just so happened to be what she was passionate about. She lit up and began to tell me about her career in software sales, the travel that she had the opportunity to do, all of the leaders she's been able to meet, and the personal and professional growth that she's experienced in her career.

I was fascinated.

She continued to tell me stories and share her passion for sales and she suddenly stopped. She looked at me dead in the eyes and said, "You know, you really have the potential to be doing more. Have you ever thought about a career in software sales?"

No.

I had never thought about a career in software sales. I knew that I wanted to do something different but had no idea what that was. Software sales? I've only sold direct to consumers. I've never sold to a business before. There's no way I could get a job in software sales.

My mind was racing with both possibility and doubt.

A few days had gone by and the thought of working in software somewhat escaped me. While sitting in my office, I heard a *ding*. I stood up to greet whoever walked in and it was that same woman.

"My company is actively looking to fill an account executive position for one of their products. Why don't you share your resume with me and I will give it to the hiring manager? Oh, and we would also like to go ahead and move forward with that apartment you showed us the other day!" she said.

"Yes, that sounds great! I need to do a few updates to my resume and I can get that to you by the end of the week! Let's get all the paperwork for your apartment started, and I will get you locked into that unit," I replied.

I went home that evening and immediately started researching the company she worked for and the product for the open position. "Oh shit," I thought, "this is like reading a foreign language. I have no idea what any of this means. I know nothing about software. I know nothing about business-to-business sales. There is no way I can do this. There is no way my resume will even get past the hiring manager. Why even go for it?"

I got to thinking a little bit more about the question "Why even go for it?" As a child, I was never afraid to go for it. To push myself outside of my comfort zone or to try something new. If I was told I couldn't do something, my response without hesitation would be "Watch me." When did this change happen?

Somewhere throughout my journey, my self-confidence had been diminished. I was looking for validation of my worth through what I've accomplished, the monthly goals I achieved, and for others to tell me that I was doing a good job. I would think things like "If I could just make partner in this company *then* I will feel worthy."

It was at that moment that I realized no one is going to come and give me validation that I am enough. That I am worthy of applying for this job and going for it. I was the only person who could give myself that permission to be powerful. And it was at that moment that I did.

There it was. That feeling. The feeling of being in my full power and having an uncompromised will. I got to work on my resume and sent it off the next day. At this point, I kind of just let go. I didn't really expect to hear anything or get an interview. I was just so proud that I overcame my own self-doubts, changed the story I was telling myself, and sent in the resume. It didn't matter what happened next.

That following week, I went on my lunch break and had a voicemail on my phone. It was from a Colorado number that I didn't recognize. "Probably a spam call," I thought to myself. But it wasn't. It was the hiring manager calling to schedule an initial interview with me for the role of an account executive! I quickly went to my car, my nerves at an all-time high, and found a good spot to park and call her back.

She answered the phone right away and asked if now was a good time to talk. "Yes, now is great!" I said. I am almost certain she could hear in my voice how nervous I was, but we both just kept the conversation going. I seemed to be making a good impression, and after answering her questions, she was excited to tell me about the hiring process and what I could expect as next steps.

I was in shock. Is this really happening? Did I really just set up an interview for next week with the VP of sales? Yes, I did!

The day had come and it was time for me to go to my interview. I changed outfits at least five times trying to find the perfect business professional look, and I fixed my hair and makeup another five times before I felt ready to walk out the door. When I got in the car and started to drive to the office, all of the doubt rushed in like someone opened the floodgates. "I am never going to get this job; I am not smart enough. What if I am not able to answer one of the interview questions? They are going to think I am a joke. This is a waste of everyone's time. I am not qualified for this job."

None of these thoughts were very beneficial to me going into this interview and doing the best I can do. None of these thoughts were even true. I am smart and I will answer whatever question is asked to the best of my ability and this is not a waste of anyone's time because I am worth the time. I've got this. I can do this and I will do this. I am going to take this chance on myself and be confident doing it.

The interview went . . . *great!* I was surprised how much of the experiences that I had in retail translated to the B2B world and how easily I was able to demonstrate how my experiences were relatable to what they were looking for in an account executive. The VP of sales was so knowledgeable that I walked out feeling very excited for the opportunity to learn from him if I were to get this job, and I really wanted this job.

Although I really wanted this particular job and to work and learn from this VP of sales, I gained more that day than the opportunity to change my career. I gained trust in myself. I gained the ability to ditch the negative thoughts, change the story, and to be in my full power. I've known all along what I am capable of; it was a matter of allowing myself to go for it and giving myself that freedom. This gift was so empowering and something that I've never forgotten.

Much to my shock and surprise, I ended up getting the job! This was the start of a totally new challenge. I had so much to learn, and it really was much like learning a completely new language. On top of that, there were many leaders in the organization who had many doubts about my ability to be successful, and they weren't shy about letting me know. But I was determined to be successful. It didn't matter what these people thought about me. I knew who I was, and I knew what I was capable of. There was no way that I was going to let other people's opinions slow me down—this was my chance.

"I can learn anything," I kept telling myself. I leveraged the technical resources that were available to the account executives, shadowed any and all sales calls I could, and picked up the phone and started talking to customers. There was no better way for me to learn than to dive right in. Within a year and a half, I went from being a woman who didn't know anything about software to a woman standing onstage in front of all her peers (and yes, those leaders who doubted me) to accept my award as top salesperson and for making President's Club.

My journey has not been one big moment that has placed me exactly where I want to be . . . yet. It has been a series of moments that have, in themselves, been huge shifts and uplevels to my career and finances.

What I've learned throughout my journey so far is that it's okay to trust myself. When I say yes to myself and I take that bet on myself, the expansion that I receive on the other side is immense. As terrifying as it can be, leaning into the most powerful version of myself is also rewarding. My story isn't over yet. As I grow, I discover areas of my life and of myself where I need to continue to lean into saying yes to the most empowered version of me.

About The Author

Brooke (Anderson)
Leggett

Brooke (Anderson) Leggett is a widely regarded sales leader with more than 10 years of professional sales experience in direct business-to-business and channel sales models. For the past 5 years, Brooke has focused on SaaS solutions for emerging technologies and driving innovation with multi-billion dollar organizations and Fortune 500 companies for a more sustainable future. She has received multiple awards for her achievements including Presidents Club and Top Sales within her organizations.

Brooke is passionate about continued personal and professional growth and encouraging others to live out their most fulfilling lives. If you would like to connect with her, you can reach out directly on LinkedIn.

Connect with Brooke:

Chapter 6

Life Requires Decisions

by Penny Cooper

LIFE IS MADE UP of a series of decisions. Sometimes we make the same decisions repeatedly—out of habit or simply because that's how we were taught.

Do you hit the snooze button again or respond to the alarm and get up ready to face the day? Do you leave the water running while brushing your teeth or turn off the faucet?

These seemingly minor decisions may only impact you in a small way. Sometimes, those seemingly inconsequential decisions accumulate over time and have a more significant impact on us than we thought.

And, occasionally, one comes to a crossroads and has an opportunity to make a monumental decision that's life-altering and legacy-making. That is what happened "for" me in February of 2012.

The life I had carefully crafted for myself and my family was about to be upended. It wasn't just a job change, or a lifestyle change, or a financial change. It was an everything change.

I was a work-from-home, solo-parenting, homeschooling mom of one son.

As an executive in the corporate offices at a Fortune 100 company, my work life was going great. I had eighteen years with the company and had worked my way up the corporate ladder into a role I loved. It almost seemed like the perfect position.

Having excelled in my career and having obtained numerous promotions, I thoroughly enjoyed the roles and responsibilities I had been given. Even though I worked fifty-plus hours a week, my work-from-home schedule was feasible for the life I had arranged for my family.

At the time, work-from-home positions were not as plentiful as they are now. As a Christian, I felt incredibly blessed by the Lord to be able to work from home and be there for my son. When he was almost twelve, my company eliminated their work-from-home policy. This news felt devastating to me.

They offered me a terrific position with an excellent salary doing something I would have been good at and enjoyed.

However, because the new position would be in New York City, it would have required over an hour commute, each way, every day, five days a week. And I would still be expected to "clock" fifty to sixty hours at the office on top of my commute time. If I took the position, I knew I would not be able to pop into my tween son's room, answer school questions during our lunch hour, or even be there to drive him to afternoon or evening activities. This change meant I would miss out on so much of his life.

Our home was our haven. We worked there, schooled there, played there, slept there. The possibility of giving up this lifestyle made me feel quite uneasy. I did not want a change in my livelihood to affect the close relationship we had built.

Many people I talked to for advice thought the decision was a no-brainer. One friend said, "Penny, you work at a great company, you have a six-figure salary, your son is old enough to take care of himself, there's a good school district right by your house, or your mom can still be there to monitor his homeschool work. You should accept the new position."

But that advice didn't just ring true for me. I didn't want such an extreme change in lifestyle for myself or my family. But more importantly, this was not what I felt called to do.

God had placed certain things on my heart for my family.

Homeschooling was high on the list. Being present for my son was monumentally important, no matter the cost to my career or our finances.

I prayed for guidance. How could I be there for my son and support my family?

I made lists of pros and cons and a "what will I do if" list.

After much prayer and consideration, peace came when I gave myself permission to lean into the role I knew I was meant for. I was a mom first. That had to be my priority.

**

In my youth, if you had asked me what my ideal life looked like, I would have told you about my cottage-style home where I homeschooled my children and lived with my devoted husband.

Sadly, not all of that dream came true. I have learned the importance of focusing on what you want to expand. As I look back, I realize that instead of focusing so hard on what I did not want to happen, I should have been more focused on the positive, on what I already had and what I wanted to create. Instead of holding on to the mantra "I am not going to get divorced," I should have focused on what I wanted: a healthy marriage, a strong faith, and a great legacy for my son. With this job offer on the table, I was at a crossroads and had an opportunity to make a monumental decision. I left my corporate job with a severance package, a mortgage, and a promise that I would be more intentional about trusting God to take care of our circumstances.

I prayed, "Ok, God, I know you will take care of us. I followed through with your prompting to turn down this career-altering position; what should I do now? If I need seven little jobs with more freedom and flexibility to replace this corporate one, I'm willing—just show me the way."

And as a solo parent and sole breadwinner, I could have caved to the pressure to "just get a job" close to home—any job with a paycheck. And many family members and friends had several well-meaning conversations with me about the best thing to do, the right thing to do, the easy thing to do—get a paycheck.

But I knew I hadn't taken a leap of faith to settle for less. God had good plans for our family. I needed to be brave enough to search them out. I had a journey ahead of me, and I was ready to move forward with purpose. I knew when I put my family first, we would be cared for and blessed.

Over the years, some of those blessings may have looked like insurmountable tragedies to outsiders. To me, mindset is essential, and from this point forward, mindset played a starring role in how I stepped into the power of being mom extraordinaire—who now happens to own several wildly successful businesses.

Being an entrepreneur was not something new to me. My mom and my dad both had entrepreneurial spirits. They created and ran several businesses as I was growing up, so I was familiar with the time, energy, and investment needed to be a successful entrepreneur.

As I looked for the next right thing, I dabbled in a few hobbies or passion projects. For a short while, I opened a living-books library for homeschooled families. Next,

I tried blogging and affiliate sales. Those didn't pay the bills but were fun and comforted me as I explored other business opportunities.

Ultimately, I landed in the travel industry space and joined a travel agency focused on Disney and family travel. I eventually opened my own travel agency because of my desire to help other families create lasting memories and experience deeper connections through travel—specifically travel to Walt Disney World.

***

Four years before my career crossroads, I gave my family a trip to Walt Disney World as a Christmas present. We planned to travel in early spring. Our trip was delayed because it became evident in January that my father's five-year battle with colon cancer was coming to an end. He passed in March of 2008. As a tribute to his life and love of family, we decided to move forward with our Disney trip and traveled in late April.

Our first visit to the Magic Kingdom left a deep impression on my heart. During our time in Orlando, we learned firsthand the extraordinary way traveling to Disney was able to unite, restore, and connect our family.

We let the magic of Disney wash over us like a healing balm. We rejoiced in spending quality time together, had deep conversations, and took lots and lots of photos.

Those photos of Mickey and friends with my mom, my Aunt Net, my sisters Julie and Kim, my son Will, and I were the way we kept the magic going—especially after the sudden and unexpected passing of my Aunt Net just one week after our return from vacation. We continue to build on these memories by returning to Disney with friends and –family—including my brother Jon, his wife Laura, and their children Emily and Jonathan. The trips with the three children are some of my absolute favorites.

As I thought about what I wanted to do, I realized I could help others, especially families, find that same contentment and enjoyment through travel.

Working at that first agency was incredibly enjoyable. It was an ideal place to learn about the travel business and connect with other like-minded businesswomen and men, many of whom were parents and shared a desire to love their kids and keep family connections close. I made some great friends at my first travel agency.

As an entrepreneur with a lifelong love of learning, continued growth and goal-setting are always at the top of my mind. I looked both in and outside of the travel industry to tap into resources that would help me improve my business skills and help me take the next steps needed to grow my business.

Several years into my travel career, I found a mentor in the travel industry who has been instrumental in my continued growth as an entrepreneur and person. She encouraged me to lean into a mindset of attraction and abundance. While she has a deep passion for helping others build successful travel businesses, she firmly believes you are best served by addressing your whole self. Through her encouragement, I grew as much on a personal level as I did as a business owner.

I know when I lean into my faith—God blesses me. So I took everything being presented to me by mentors and coaches and allowed prayer and the Bible to be my filters as I determined the right path. And then, I acted on promptings and moved forward.

Another pivotal moment in my journey happened when I realized even though I had made a monumental life change, I was still "playing it safe" because I was content with just enough.

The desire to honor the growth opportunities in store for me led me to make bold moves in partnership with a travel peer. Unfortunately, that particular partnership did not last, and in less than eight months, I was confronted with making further unexpected business moves. This change was incredibly difficult as it meant the loss of personal friendships as well as momentum in my business. While devastating at the time, I now know this setback was the catalyst for the success of my current endeavors.

Along the way, there were also difficult financial times when I wasn't sure how I would pay the bills or even how I would be able to buy groceries. Remember when I told God I would work seven jobs? Well, for a while, I thought that promise was going to come to fruition. Let's just say for a couple of years, I had four or five 1099s for my tax return. These financial woes, and my experiences at the first and second agencies, were all lessons on my continued journey to be a more powerful person. Looking back, I appreciate those opportunities and can see how they prepared me to find the fantastic business partner I now have in my business.

Making decisions and pursuing growth through mindset has continued to help me flourish.

As I outlined this chapter, I wrote down several vital phrases I've learned from various mentors and coaches over the years.

Each phrase has marked a turning point in my life and helped me grow by pushing me forward one step at a time.

"What you focus on expands."

"What you resist persists."

"Don't compare your Chapter Two to someone else's Chapter Twenty."

"You get to want what you want."

"Take inspired action."

"Everything is working out for you, even when it seems like it's not."

"You are either winning or learning."

Out of context, you may think of these as fortune cookie wisdom. However, when applied to my life circumstances, I see them as stepping stones. They encouraged me to envision a bigger, better picture for my future. The understanding that came with each teaching allowed me to make powerful decisions.

One of the best pieces of advice I gleaned from a mentor was "Don't be afraid to put yourself in the room with successful people."

If I earned my way into the room, that's great; however, if I needed to buy my way into the room, I would do that too. I pay membership fees, and I join mastermind groups because I want to be around successful people.

I want to see what they're doing. I want to hear what they're saying. I want to understand how they got where they are and how they've crafted their success.

Spending time with successful people motivates, inspires, and challenges me.

As an introvert, being in a room with successful people easily stretches me out of my comfort zone. These groups have led to opportunities for me to speak onstage, present my ideas, and receive accolades for what I am doing in the industry. That is very affirming and continues to motivate me to press forward.

I know I am even more powerful when I give myself permission to invest in myself this way.

When you think about investing, you usually consider the potential ROI (Return on Investment) to know whether or not the investment is a solid choice. During a recent coaching session, I described investing as figuring out "if the juice is worth the squeeze."

When I invest in myself, the ROI I most often see is increased confidence. This confidence, in turn, inspires others, including my son. And hopefully, my future generations will be beneficiaries of the legacy-building choices I confidently make in my businesses every day.

It was in one of these amazing groups that I met my current business partner. And because of our successful partnership, we have grown two six-figure businesses, in addition to our individual travel agencies. We've developed a team of like-minded women, helping them be their best selves and fulfilling their dreams as entrepreneurs.

I describe the relationship between my current business partner and myself as a puzzle piece. We fit each other. Instead of C Level titles, we describe our company roles as Visionary and Integrator. We are enough alike that we have a true friendship. We complement each other in ways that allow us each to do more of what we love doing as entrepreneurs. She is brilliant and unconditionally strives to help boost those around her to reach their full potential. I feel fortunate to work alongside someone who also brings out the best in me.

***

I'm writing this chapter in 2023, so it has been more than ten years since I left my corporate position and started that first travel agency. I fulfilled my quest to homeschool my son from kindergarten through high school. He graduated, earned his Eagle Scout award, and now attends a major university on the East Coast. And his dreams are also coming true, as this summer, he is interning with his favorite major league baseball team and hopes to start his career with them after graduation. I am proud of all he has accomplished—all we have accomplished together.

My mom, who helped homeschool my son, is and will always be my loyal confidant and adviser. As she lives with us, I am the definition of the sandwich generation. I have responsibilities for both sides of the family, and I wouldn't want it any other way. Being a mom alongside and with my mom is a blessing I will always treasure.

After ten years of self-employment, I have learned to be content no matter the circumstances, but I also know that living by faith doesn't mean you have to live your life in survival mode. I believe God wants me and my family to thrive.

In fact, I can be an immense blessing to others, curate a better family legacy, and bring more glory to God when I strive to be the best version of myself by living an abundant and authentic life.

I know when a break is needed, there will be a respite. When finances are required, they are supplied. When faith is necessary, an opportunity to be faithful presents itself.

And when I'm open to it, growth and abundance await me, and the blessings become generational.

About The Author

Penny Cooper

Penny Cooper is an award-winning entrepreneur and the founder of Embrace the Magic Travel, a travel agency dedicated to helping travelers celebrate life through their vacations. Her agency offers tailor-made itineraries designed to foster deeper connections and lasting memories for the whole family.

With over a decade of experience and hundreds of families served, she is an esteemed leader in the travel industry who loves helping families create vacation memories with extra style and savvy.

She is a member of the American Society of Travel Advisors, the Virtuoso Family & Celebration Travel community, and several travel masterminds. Penny is a frequent guest speaker for industry & agency events, was a recurring panelist at the Book More Travel Workshop, and has won several travel industry awards.

As a lifelong learner, she has a keen interest in marketing and lead generation.

She is widely regarded by the Disney and Family Travel Industry for her use of email automation, providing unparalleled customer experience and deeper client connection through storytelling. This led her to co-found Magic Made Simple, a media company that specializes in written-for-you content for busy travel professionals to attract, nurture, and care for clients with their own personal sparkle!

Through Magic Made Simple, she encourages her fellow travel advisors to share their personal stories, deepen the loyalty of their clients, and solidify their expert status.

Penny believes every day is a day to celebrate. You will find her putting sprinkles on everything, using her best china and the fancy napkins, and making memories with her family.

Connect with Penny:

Chapter 7

Choosing Joy

by Johanna White

IN ONE NIGHT, I went from being healthy and ultrafit to partially paralyzed on the left side with collapsed vocal cords and food coming out of my nose instead of going down my throat when I tried to swallow. And it happened without warning, or even without visible reason. My whole world flipped upside down, and I went from a life of safe, self-prescribed certainty, to one where all of the results were "inconclusive," and the only thing I knew for sure was that I actually didn't know anything. At all.

Now, looking back on that experience, I can say without a doubt that my greatest obstacle became my greatest catalyst for me stepping into the epic life that I was made for! The journey has not always been easy, but I have learned to turn those challenges into opportunities to serve others. I have learned to punch fear in the face, *do* something about what I believe, and to never take the doctor's word as the last word.

Most of the people who know me today would say that I'm an adventure-loving badass, who seizes the moment (not just one moment—all the moments!) and who doesn't let anything resembling fear hold her back from living life full out. And they would be right. Now. But that was not always the case.

For the first twenty-five years of my life, fear drove the bus. I played everything safe, always made the healthy choices, and did everything "right." I flew under the radar in every way that I could (I thought that complete and total invisibility was a small price to pay to avoid having haters at all costs) and was more or less content to live a safe, if somewhat uninspiring, life. But then one day, out of nowhere, a brain tumor diagnosis turned my world upside down.

This story starts in fall of 2013, back when I was at a very low-income job, barely making enough to pay the bills. I was working at a small creative services agency, so I *was* doing design and technically working in my field, but in the lowest form of design that could exist—checking ads for errors before they went to press. If that wasn't uninspiring enough, it was a really toxic culture, and you never knew if you were gonna get fired from one day to the next.

But I was scared of trying for bigger things because I was afraid to fail. I was even *more* afraid that the agencies I might apply to would see me and confirm my worst secret fear—that my design skills weren't actually all that great (and I was no prize either.) So, bowing to that ever-present impostor syndrome, I let the old anxiety soundtrack keep whispering in my ear with thoughts like: "You're just lucky to have a job in your field. The design market is flooded. Blah, blah, excuse, blah." I was fully stuck in a mindset of mediocre and not going anywhere anytime soon!

And then, out of the blue, my safe (but very small) life was interrupted.

In the middle of the night, I woke up to a migraine from hell. It lasted three days, and when it finally went away, I experienced sudden partial paralysis on the left side of my face, my vocal cords were paralyzed, I couldn't swallow, and my sternocleidomastoid muscle atrophied completely overnight.

Breathing was hard.

I couldn't talk.

Food was coming out of my nose rather than going down my throat. I don't want to get too gory with the details, but I also want to quickly explain the severity of this traumatic experience. Because when my health took a turn for the worst, it was a turning point for me in a *big way*. I realized that though I had dreamed of living up to my potential someday, that "someday" would always be tomorrow unless I did something today to make a change. And suddenly, tomorrow wasn't guaranteed. Two weeks after the official diagnosis, I looked around at my utterly non-impactful work and felt determination rise up inside. I did *not* come this far to only come *this far*. I refused to die without ever even tapping into my potential.

With so much unknown surrounding the brain tumor, I decided that I wanted to do work that mattered with the time I had left, so just a few weeks after the diagnosis, I quit my job (without much of a plan beyond figuring it out as I went along). I literally walked out the door and down the street, knocking on business doors, Mary Kay-ing my way into owning my own design business. I was the stranger knocking on the door of your office introducing myself and saying, "Hi! I'm Jo, and I design stuff. Do you need stuff designed?"

Whoever said door-to-door sales were dead?

I filed my first LLC for Design by Jo with only eight hours of freelance graphic design and website work officially booked on the clock. It turns out that having nothing left to lose will go a *long* way in slapping a piece of duct tape over the voice of fear in your head and unleashing your inner warrior.

I started two more businesses within those first few months after diagnosis and gave myself plenty to look forward to on the other side of this tumor because I had already decided that there *was* going to be more life for me to live. And I needed to have more to think about besides the broken record in my head of "You're going to die. You're going to die. You're going to die."

The health side of this journey was not easy, and I bounced from surgeon to surgeon for two and a half years, with doctor after doctor doing MRIs, only to tell me again that the results were inconclusive. Well . . . they were conclusively deciding that I needed surgery, while also all saying that *they* didn't have the right equipment/experience/team to be the one to do so, but they were sure the next guy would be just the doctor that I needed. Even the brain biopsy produced the same non-answer answers time after time: "The results are inconclusive." What does one do with that kind of news? It was frustrating to say the least.

Before the tumor, I had been a fit and very active person, and one who easily turned physical effort into muscles. But now, the pounding cardio workouts that I loved so much became unbearable due to the pain in my head, and even more frustrating was the fact that no matter how many workouts I did, my body went the other direction, getting weaker rather than stronger. This sudden lack of results in the only area I had ever felt good at frustrated me to the point of giving up on movement altogether. If the workouts weren't going to work by making me strong and healthy again, then what the heck was the point? I might as well just give up, lick my wounds, and curl up on the couch and eat Doritos until I died.

Trying to stay positive in a situation such as this felt impossible, but I've never been one to stay down and defeated for long. Plus, my determination had been unlocked, and my mind was becoming powerful. I decided that every single day I was still able to move was a gift, and if I could move at all, I was going to—whether it made my muscles stronger or not. Movement itself was the gift, and my new motto became: "I can, so I will."

Looking back though, I wouldn't have been able to do it without a great friend of ours who showed up on my doorstep the day after my diagnosis to give me the gift of an iPad, with every healing scripture he could find downloaded on it. He handed it to me and told me this was a tool for the battle, and that we were going to fight! In my darkest moment, when I was tempted to go curl up and lick my wounds and die, or at least to share my sad tale of sick body woe with anyone who would listen, he challenged me to take a different approach. He reminded me that for my whole life I had said that "I believed in God and that I believed in healing" and this was my chance to act like I actually meant what I had said.

I was *so* angry with him at first, telling him about all the people who I had seen die, even though they said they believed in healing too. And saying how I didn't want to be a faker—I didn't want to go around telling people that everything was perfect when it clearly wasn't. But he gently reminded me that their stories were not my story. That I was the author of my story, and this was my chance to write a different ending—but that it would all come down to the words I would speak to my own self, and to the world.

I accepted the challenge.

I figured, "What's the worst that can happen?" If I went around talking about how I was getting better and was healed and then I "up and died" anyway, I guess I would look like a fool. But if that happened, who cares! I would be too dead to be bothered about looking stupid. But if he was right, *if I was the author of my own story, and the beliefs I held and the words I used truly determined my outcome,* then I had nothing to lose, and everything to gain.

Through this journey I learned just how powerful our minds can be in healing *or* in re-succumbing to symptoms (I had both outcomes happen a few times before I finally put two and two together.) I began to notice how when I was anxious and fearful about the situation, the symptoms would nearly double. And I also noticed that the few times I could finally take my mind away from thinking about the pain in my head, it would actually fade for a bit.

But nothing cemented the power of our thoughts in my mind quite so clearly as the day that I showed up to one of my six-month MRI checkups almost fully healed (symptoms had reversed, even the ones the doctors had said were permanent due to nerve damage). But then, when I received the new scan from the doctor showing that the mass was still there as big as ever, I left in tears and woke up the next morning with all of my symptoms back plus some new ones! That day, I almost made the terrible mistake of taking the doctor's word as the last word.

But thankfully, in that moment when I woke up with previously healed symptoms back in full force, it finally clicked that *the fear of this tumor was killing me almost as much as the tumor itself,* and though I didn't know yet if I could actually do anything about the tumor, I *knew* I could do something about the fear.

If you've ever tried to tell yourself to simply not be afraid, then you know how much that approach does *not* work. The more you focus on not having fear, the more afraid you get. So I gave up on trying to kick it to the curb, and instead just began to drown it out. When my own thoughts wanted to stay on the hamster wheel of "you're going to die," then I replaced them with intentional positive inputs instead. Sometimes, if you don't feel like you have enough faith to get through the next moment, then it is time to borrow someone else's.

Once I realized I could actually do something about the fear, and fully drown it out, *then* I was finally able to turn my attention back to my body. I found every input about healing that I could and put it into my mind all day long, every day. I played healing Scriptures while I was trying to ignore the pounding in my head and fall asleep. I played sermons and training about healing while I worked. I took every single verse that my friend had saved on that little iPad, and I spoke it out to myself, out loud, all day long. When someone asked how I was doing, I spoke very carefully, filling them in on what the doctors said was going on, without claiming the doctors' statements as my ultimate outcome. And what do you know, it worked!

It didn't happen overnight, and there were no sudden flash-of-light miracles like I always wanted. But as I continued to choose to believe in my healing despite any and all physical evidence to the contrary, my body started to believe it too. My life became a series of tiny miracles, and every morning I had to make the choice to keep collecting evidence of my healing and see it through, no matter what thoughts or discouraging symptoms came up to the contrary.

One day I would notice that it had been two or three days without a headache. Soon I noticed that I could talk at full volume again and that I could eat solid food without choking. Next, I noticed that the atrophied muscle in my neck was fully visible again (despite the doctors believing that the nerve damage causing the atrophy would be permanent, even if they were able to do surgery.) My symptoms started getting better and better and better, until my body once again functioned at full capacity!

And it turned out that drowning out the fear with new thoughts became one of the most important steps toward healing that I could take. Now I know that taking those steps was the only thing I could truly control—I couldn't force the outcome, but I could take the action of changing the inputs.

Mind you, there were still *no* doctors willing to operate on this tumor at this point. However, the shining clarity came when I realized that I didn't actually fear death . . . but rather I feared losing my quality of life and mobility that I was used to and, therefore, losing my happiness in the process. But then I realized that even in moments of extreme pain when my body didn't work like I thought it should, I was still able to *choose* joy in that moment. And if I could, in fact, choose joy at any time, in any circumstance, then I had nothing left to fear.

It turns out that the certainty that I had clung to my whole life (and sacrificed everything for) was actually just an illusion, and that choosing joy was a powerful antidote to the uncertainty and fear that had been running the show for so long. Even though the doctors were not able to help this time, my faith in God, my belief in healing, and my utter determination to finally take relentless action *on* that belief kept me going. The tumor is gone, and I am stronger than when I started.

I gave myself permission to be powerful. I could move, so I did.

I could be joyful, so I was going to be.

I learned that what you believe matters, but what you do about what you believe matters even more.

I didn't want to live my life as just a survivor—I wanted to *thrive*.

After the brain tumor healed, I turned this newfound discovery about the power of belief in myself and what was truly possible onto my business. I now knew the importance of taking action on what you believe, so I leaned into helping my clients actually *do* something about their belief that they had something of massive value to offer the world and actually step into *showing* that belief through their brand. I expanded my offerings beyond just visual design and began helping them tell their story and their "why" for their businesses so that together we could create a powerful brand by design rather than by default.

I finally started showing up for myself and living the life God intended me to live. Life is too short to live it as anybody else, and I'm going all in as who He made me to be. In that, I get to live up to my potential and help my clients do the same.

Now I'm on a mission to help other driven founders fully capture their uniqueness and embody their limitless potential.

My journey has been challenging to be sure, but now I know that challenges can be opportunities to serve others, and I am grateful for every day I get to make a difference.

About The Author

Johanna White

Johanna White is an award-winning graphic designer, visual branding strategist, and the founder of Design By Jo Studio, where she believes that if someone is the best at what they do, they deserve to look like it! For the past decade, she's worked with individuals, startups, and Fortune 200 brands worldwide to help them magnetize their dream opportunities, clients, and investors, and to be as delightfully expensive as they deserve to be.

Johanna knows there's no limit to success, and she proved it several years ago when she took life by the horns and started three companies within one year while battling a brain tumor. At a time when everyone else in her life was suggesting that she quit working and go on social security to cover medical bills, she chose to do the opposite and defy the odds. As a result, Johanna is now a "Dreamer Extraordinaire" for top performers, elite experts, and companies who are driven to maximize their impact.

Thanks to her "now or never" approach to life, she finds fresh inspiration from balancing work with play, and is just as likely to be found designing her client's brands from the top of a mountain with a snowboard strapped to her feet, or from a beachside chair in the Dominican as from her desk. A lover of experiencing life to the fullest, she spends her weekends on her motorcycle, ballroom dancing, or riding her horse Romeo as he charms the internet with videos of his sweet puppy dog demeanor.

These days, Johanna is on a mission to help other driven founders fully capture their uniqueness, level up their legacy, and embody their limitless potential with the power of their brand!

Connect with Johanna:

Chapter 8

Powerful in Faith

by Drea Buer

PERMISSION TO BE POWERFUL was never about what I thought it was.

It wasn't about making a stand for myself. It wasn't about doing something that will be heard around the world. It wasn't about what I can do to leave a legacy that will be remembered for years to come.

The permission to be powerful was all about filling the hole of that empty feeling. It's been about finding that reason to wake up in the morning with thankfulness and being grateful for another day no matter what life throws at you. It has been about appreciating what we have currently and living life with the most joy because of it. It's been about learning what my true potential is and what I was put on this earth to be and do.

The permission to be powerful didn't lie in my hands at all.

But the permission to be powerful was inside me all along!

I just needed to receive it.

For much of my life, I have lived as a "good person." I accepted Christ as my Lord and Savior when I was fourteen, I was baptized, I went to church, volunteered, made decent moral decisions (according to society's standards) when I could, I asked for forgiveness when those decisions weren't so great, and kept on living life large, trying to be that "good" person I was meant to be.

I'm guessing this might be resonating with you as you read this, and I'm here to tell you that I *still* struggled just about every day, because I felt there was something missing. I felt there was something more in me that had yet to be tapped into, and I had no idea what that was or how to do it. I knew I had more potential, but what was it?

When I made my decision to expand into the unknown and start working with a coach and building a business, this was the first time I did anything for me. All my life I have wanted to make other's dreams come true rather than making my own come true. Most likely it was due to the lack of belief I had in myself when it was so much easier to believe in someone else and knowing failure was not an option for them, because they had me. Wow, presumptuous, right? Believe it or not, I truly felt this way. I knew that I would do *anything* to help make their dreams come true. If only I could have applied that worth to myself earlier on! With making this decision to "bet on me," I was going against my own grain and gave myself the permission to stop wondering once and for all and give it all I've got to see what I'm made of and be open to any and all possibilities along the way.

The floodgates burst open, and I wasn't even sure what I had in my boat. Did I even have a boat? Too many of us can relate when I say I did—and at times still do—play the what-if game, but quickly, I was able to turn it into a "What if I succeed?"

I didn't know what to expect, but as soon as the decision was made, I was quickly surrounded by a support system of wonderful people and a handful of women in a mastermind who had similar beliefs, passions, and goals that easily and quickly turned into some amazing friendships.

I probably read more books than in my entire college career during this time, and I wanted to name a few as they were incredibly impactful on my journey from where I was to where I am today. Starting with *The Power of One More* by Ed Mylett. This book was sent to me as a surprise gift from a friend. It was the encouragement I needed to go that extra mile and not be afraid and put that same belief I had always put into others into myself. After this book, I knew that I had the grit and passion it takes to be great!

I then read *The Science of Getting Rich* by Wallace D. Wattles. This book was the "ah-ha" moment I needed. Contrary to popular belief, there is plenty of wealth and happiness to go around. God did not intend for us to live in poverty. He wants you to be rich and joyful! Then the doozy. It was suggested I read *Ask and It Is Given* by Esther and Jerry Hicks. This one was powerful and scary in so many ways. I'll come back to this in a moment.

"Keep an open mind" was my mantra through the start of this journey, and it was still very much in play at this point. Fast forward to this amazing, life-changing business retreat in Sedona, Arizona. I remember calling up Brady (my husband) and telling him to prepare himself, because I was coming home a brand-new woman! My time there will never be forgotten for many reasons:

- I was empowered and energized to be better and strive for bigger goals.

- I met women who were on the same "wavelength" as me. You could talk about visions, spiritual warfare, and dreams and not feel like you were the odd man out or making others uncomfortable.

- During the retreat, I also discovered that I had a few things I needed to work on: not relying on anyone else's permission to go for the goals I set; forgiveness; and acknowledging I had a problem with receiving.

I will always laugh with astonishment at the moment at this retreat when I was midsentence, asking Elyse a question about who I wanted to serve as my target niche in my business—basically asking "for permission" (and not for the first time). That is when I stopped myself and said (with the most respect and love), "Why am I asking you?

I don't need your permission to decide this." Imagine Gru from *Despicable Me* chiming in at this very moment and saying, "Light bulb!" This was a moment that I will cherish forever. The personal validation into believing and trusting who I am and what I am capable of finally came to light. In a way, it was the movement from me being "the sales rep" and always needing permission to make big moves, to "the boss" of my own company and the decision maker. That's a big deal!

We then had a fantastic guest speaker/singer, Toni Jones, who came in hot with her positive affirmations and what that can do for the soul. She started to sing about forgiveness and when I say the waterworks started, it was a waterfall, y'all. Mind you, anyone who knows me knows I cry for all the happy, all the sad, sometimes the scared—but the emotions are robust in this soul and they don't mind showing themselves when they feel the need. Understanding that this hit a nerve, I started questioning myself, "*What? Why?* Have I not forgiven the people of the past that altered my life in one way or another? Have I not forgiven myself in any of these instances? Why did that hit so hard?"

The last hurdle to make its presence was on receiving. Wow. The *power* in receiving and the problem I didn't know I had! I'm writing this wondering how many of you are like me. You can give and give all day long and not expect anything in return and be so happy about it, but when the day comes that you have to receive something in return? This is when it gets hard. You are actually awkward about it because you're not sure how to receive it. In fact, sometimes it just plum gives you anxiety! Turns out, I've been trying to avoid "receiving" all my life! I was the girl on a date that paid for the meal or activity (or at least tried) to avoid any feeling of obligation to the other person *just in case.* This concept was applied to strangers, friends, or even family—I did this with everyone I knew and didn't even realize it until now and little did I know it was only the beginning of what the true meaning and beauty of what receiving really was all about.

Since I drove down to Arizona, audiobooks were very welcomed for what turned into a twenty-two-hour drive home back to Wyoming with the wonderful winter weather. I learned that there were two books by Abraham Hicks and thought, "Well . . . can't hurt to listen to these while I drive back rather than reading them when I get back home." So that's exactly what I did. Want to know the weirdest part? My heart hurt the *entire* time I was listening to these books.

Have you ever had that feeling? Something you hear or something happens that pains you so deeply your heart hurts? I've learned that not everyone knows of this feeling, but trust me when I say, it's a very real thing and I know I'm not alone in knowing this feeling. I didn't know what it was from. I thought maybe the stress of all the snowstorms in my two-wheel drive Malibu Barbie was causing it.

I wanted to bring you back to this book, *Ask and It Is Given*, because there's a lot here to unpack. The idea behind this book is that Abraham Hicks is a spiritual being that is being channeled through a woman, Esther Hicks. Remember how I said it was powerful yet scary? It was powerful in the sense that I was able to grab positives out of reading this book (I believe, due to the foundation I already had built in my faith) because I put the "person" who wrote it out of mind and dove into what the book had to offer. It was scary because I had to grapple the entire time with whether I fundamentally agreed with the entire concept of a spirit speaking through a human. But from this book, I dove deeper into the understanding that God wants to have a relationship with us and we shouldn't be afraid to ask Him for what we want. We do have to understand that God is always going to answer prayers in His time and with His will in mind, but He wants us to ask so that He can bless us and give us what we need. Then we have the choice of receiving those blessings/answered prayers however they may come. It's what a most beautiful relationship embodies; conversations, guidance, trust, faith, and love, all wrapped into those three main points.

Remember that heart pain I was talking about? I was still trying to figure it out. I followed activities others instructed me to try to learn what it might be from. None of them hit right. Was this pain from what was bothering me in my forgiveness journey? Was it due to my lack of receiving? I tried making up what it could be multiple times. I tried convincing myself it was one of these things because I was tired of trying to figure it out. I was tired of not knowing what this was and why it was holding on . . . lo and behold, each and every time, the reason I was trying to force wasn't the answer.

From the very beginning, I wrestled with this concept of a spirit "speaking through a human" and whether it was good or not. I even stated out loud in my discussions with Brady, "If I believe that demons can possess people, why can't I believe that angels can speak through people too?" I even chose not to discuss this with my parents because I did not want them to immediately shoot down this new concept that I am "keeping an open mind to" just because it might be new and maybe something that makes them uncomfortable. I asked a few people here and there about their thoughts on the subject and if they've ever heard of Abraham Hicks; not many have heard about them specifically but knew of "other spirits" that channeled through (or spoke through) one person or another.

I kid you not when I say I was wrestling with this idea of "something doesn't seem right here" and "keep an open mind." This keeps going on for a while, but there is more to the story.

At the height of all of this, I also started and completed *The 40 Day Prosperity Plan* by John Randolph Price. I would say it taught me to think about, ponder on, and meditate on what it's truly like to have to live with Christ within you, what that means, and how life changes because of it.

To be honest, I never knew how small I made God until this year (2023). I never knew that I was not giving him the credit He deserved for all that I have in this life. I never knew how hateful and resentful I was of the way I had lived life in the past. I never knew how poor of a relationship I had with God in general. I certainly don't have space to write about it here, but there is pure truth in how life and death are in the power of the tongue, and those who love it shall eat its fruit (Proverbs 18:21).

Remember, God does not intend for us to live in poverty. God intends for us to live a prosperous life!

The 40 Day Prosperity Plan by John Randolph Price came into play next. This meditation for forty days straight is like the meditation version of a 75 Hard workout commitment. I failed doing this the first time because I forgot a day, and it says to do this meditation every day for forty days without fail, so the second time was a charm with this one!

Listening every single day about how God is my source for everything in this life was powerful. It's not the money. It's not the people. It's not the things I have. It's not the things I do. It's all God.

One of my favorite pieces of this content was hearing how God has no knowledge of lack. Why would He? Sequentially, when you make the choice to open up your heart and live with the divine within you, you too live with no lack! Forty days and forty nights I did this meditation and journaling on how God lives within me and how I can "see" it in my life and "feel" it. The same power that healed the sick, made the blind see, rose from the dead, parted the seas—*this* is the power that lives *in* me as a child of God if *only I choose to receive it!* This was what I needed to learn in order to receive! This relationship with God that I only *thought* I knew. No longer do I hold God, or my faith, in a tiny box. No longer will I be afraid of the wonderfully big universe our God created. No longer will I be living my life my way, but God's way! Spending this time with God *every day* broadened my knowledge of what God was truly capable of and changed my mindset drastically.

At this moment in my journey, I knew what all of this "pain" was about and the reason for turmoil in my heart. It was simple; I personally did not align with Abraham Hicks and who they are. As soon as I made that realization, the pain no longer existed. I immediately felt strong in who I am and my relationship with God. It felt GOOD! However, this book challenged me in more ways than one. It also challenged me to ask myself, "Why am I so afraid to ask God for something and accept that He is willing to give it to me with no strings attached?" Thankfully, I trusted myself and I trusted my faith in God and because of this, I was able to broaden my horizons. Remember those limiting beliefs I was talking about earlier and how I changed it to "What if I succeed?" Well, I've already won. With my firm foundation in God and knowing that He is in control and wants my business and personal life to flourish . . . I have succeeded. I felt WHOLE.

As I stated at the very beginning, I've been living a life that was good but incomplete. I did all the "right things" to live the way a "Christian" should. I said the right verses, I read the Bible, I talked to others about God, I asked for forgiveness when I needed to, but I was not living up to my full potential, my full power, the full intention of what God created me to be. I can honestly say that I now know that I have never received the Father, the Son, and the Holy Ghost to live in me as I have now.

BAM! Life changed. I hear music differently. I feel (emotions) differently. I talk to people differently.

I read the Bible differently. My whole being is different.

I have heard the phrase before that accepting Christ is like getting hit by a Mack Truck. It's not enough that you believe that He sent His son to this earth to save us and die for our sins, and He rose from the dead so that we can live eternally in heaven. One factor that we forget (I did anyway) is to receive that power. It is a genuine conscious act. It is physical. When you receive Christ in your heart, everywhere you go—He goes. Every step you take—He takes it with you. Every prayer you say—is a conversation He is having *with you.* Every person you touch, God is touching them too. It's a whole new relationship. Just like how you cannot be hit by a Mack Truck and not visually see the impact it has had on your body physically, mentally, and emotionally—there would be *no question* that you just got run over—there is *no question* that your spirit has been changed indefinitely.

I have said it before, but I never knew what this meant until this year! This is a big deal! A life-changing experience to say the very least. When I am asked about this change, people want to know what happened. What did I do? How did I change? I didn't do anything other than pay attention to the nudges, be willing to look deep inside myself to answer the questions that would pop up, and listen to what God has to tell me. I also make it more of a nonnegotiable when considering spending time with God on the daily, whether that be through reading, prayer, listening, or singing, and I can tell you that I look forward to it every day. Not making anything else my source of success other than God himself. This is really what the true permission to be powerful comes down to. Can you imagine the impact I can have in helping others make their dreams come true now? Standing tall, proud, and confident in my own –skin—my own being. That was all I wanted in the past. Now that I've given myself permission to be powerful in reaching for my own dreams, I am going to be able to help others in a way that is more special than ever before!

I know that I did not need anyone's permission but my own to accept God into my life and live with His power surging through me. I know that my forgiveness wasn't due to anything or anyone of the past but more about not knowing that I had been missing out on a greater relationship with Christ all this time. I also know that I had learned to receive, and I just received the most precious gift I could ever ask for . . . living in Christ.

I have tried to stand without power before. I have tried to build my own life with my own brick-and-mortar. I have tried being angry and not caring about the outcomes of my actions. All this and more is constantly in the works in my life (be sure to connect with me somehow through one or more avenues of the digital ecosystem to keep up on how it is going). But a choice has been made. I surrender everything. I want to change the world! I want to sing His song and I know all of that revival's got to start with me and my permission to be powerful in Christ!

About The Author

Drea Buer

Drea's path from a modest small town to embracing a world under God's watch has been both deeply personal and relatably universal. Her life, with its joys and despairs, mirrors the imperfect humanity that is familiar to us all. Navigating through emotions from anger to love, and behaviors from harsh to gentle, Drea represents a reality many of us understand all too well.

Her spiritual journey, notably through the personal trial of divorce, brought moments of rebellion against God. Her frustration, sometimes displayed as open defiance during prayer, marks a notable chapter in her spiritual story. However, each time she strayed, Drea found herself welcomed back by God's unwavering grace and love. These experiences fortified her belief in never being alone under the gaze of a caring God.

Now, Drea embarks on a collaborative book project, intertwining her story with those of other resilient women. Here, she openly shares HER STORY about navigating from a place of powerlessness to finding her strength, particularly through the peace found in God's grace.

While the story thus far provides a window into Drea's past, her chapter in this collaboration signifies a milestone — a reflection of where she has arrived after traversing through challenges. Drea stands here, a testament to fulfilling a divine purpose, contributing her piece to a collective narrative that echoes a singular message of power, grace, and divine purpose.

Connect with Drea:

Chapter 9

From Fear to Freedom

by Leslie Thornton

BRAVERY WAS ALWAYS MY middle name. I was known as being a very courageous girl. I did things like skydiving and public speaking and other adventurous activities. But when it came to doing things where it was one hundred percent my responsibility to do those things—for example, I never had any desire to learn how to skydive without someone on my back—I was terrified.

I didn't trust myself.

So there I was, working as an ICU nurse in Albany, New York, and I was anxious as all get out. I have never felt that level of fear so regularly in my life. I was a fantastic nurse when I worked in the kidney transplant unit prior to the ICU, but in the ICU—with all of the wires and patients being unconscious and emergency pressurized situations—I was terrified of making a mistake. I was terrified of getting yelled at by the surgeons and having my mistake cost someone's life. I did fine. I got good feedback, but during lunchtime in the break room, I was reading spiritual texts, trying to do anything that I could to support myself in not feeling so anxious. Nothing was working. It had been nine months.

During this stressful time in my life, I sought out meditation. I found a tantric meditation class close to my apartment in Albany. At the end of the class, full of silent meditation and mantra singing, the group would openly discuss anything that came up for them or anything that was present for them at the time. I was moved by the openness and the heartfelt connection that these people were sharing. This opened something up for me. I began meditating twice a day for twenty minutes. At the same time, I was also on the hunt for a career change. I wanted to do something that I absolutely loved waking up and doing every single day. I didn't want to experience dread, anger, sadness, and exhaustion. I wanted to serve. In a way that felt right to me.

I was going to school to become a mental health nurse practitioner, and around the same time, I stumbled upon the world of coaching. I was obsessed. I loved the positive psychology aspect. I loved that it was actually a helpful way to create change for other human beings and completely transform their lives. I loved that I could work with people internationally as world travel was something always important to me on my list. Coaching was checking all the boxes.

In the process of becoming a coach, I had a coach. Her name was Ola and she lived in Poland and used to live in the United States. As I was working through my anxiety and fear around my nursing job, trying to figure out what I really wanted to do for the rest of my life, I asked Ola—who was a career coach—what to do.

Ola asked me two questions: "Leslie, what is something major that you have overcome in your life, or what is something you've always had a knack for?"

Immediately, what came to my mind was the fact that I got over my obsession with weight loss, using hypnosis. Immediately, Ola said, "Well I already want that! So you should probably do that!"

In my coaching certification program, I needed to coach for sixty hours in order to get certified. There was a forum to offer your coaching, so I listed that I could do hypnosis for weight loss coaching, and I had many people sign up.

Initially, I was just coaching people about how to get emotionally and mentally free from food, body, and weight. I would share my experience that hypnosis had on me. One day a practice client of mine said, "Leslie, I don't want you to tell me about the hypnosis. I actually want you to do the hypnosis on me."

At the time, the coaching was just over the phone, and I had absolutely no idea how to hypnotize anyone. But I remembered what the hypnosis was like for me and so I said, "Well heck, we're here to practice—let me give it a shot and see what happens."

The next week when I met up with this client again, she came to the phone excited and said, "Whatever you did last week, do it again. I've never felt more free around food, body, and weight in my life!"

Did this actually work? Does hypnosis actually work over the phone? Maybe I needed to become a hypnotherapist! I did some research and it turns out that hypnosis does work over the phone, and many hypnotherapists use it in that way. I also started getting curious about the science behind hypnosis and how it actually worked—and worked so well. Needless to say, my passion for helping people in this incredible way was becoming my bigger and bigger passion in life.

As I continued hating my nursing job, the anxiety seemed to get bigger the more my passion rose. Every single day off I was constantly on other coaches' webinars, learning everything that I could coaching other people and having them coach me. I was still going for my master's degree, but now I was at a point with my nursing job where I had to make a decision.

I did get my first initial client doing hypnosis for weight loss who was willing to pay me one thousand dollars for the hypnosis and support. I had proven that I could make money on my own. But how could I walk away from the retirement? How could I walk away from the health insurance? The same way that I was terrified the moment I had to bungee jump and step off that ledge in New Zealand, I was beyond scared to make the leap of faith and trust that I could leave my job that I hated and start doing something that I loved.

I was still consistent with my meditation practice. When I say that I was anxious for the full nine months that I was working in the ICU, I really meant it. It was miserable. I wondered if I should give up going for my master's to become a nurse practitioner, or give up my job that was helping me pay for my master's degree. What about health insurance? What about 401(k)s? These were the questions that paralyzed me and made me unable to act.

Meditation supported me through this really stressful time in my life. I was sitting on my bed and the sun was beaming in—it was comfortable and warm, and I was ready to meditate. As I got deeper into my meditation, something suddenly happened. The only way I could describe it was that it was a download, and quick as a flash I heard this voice that came from within my body that was not my voice—it was not me, it was not of me, and it said, "Thy will be done."

It was like a lightning bolt hit my body without any of the pain. I knew in that moment that it was time for me to go. I wasn't brave enough to make that decision at a time in my life when I did not have enough faith that the universe had in me—that God had in me. And so, something was allowed to come through me to give me that nudge that I needed to make a decision that would allow me to be happier in my life now.

My transition out of the hospital was not an easy one. I wasn't met with appreciation or support but rather anger and even hatred. After all, I had just wasted all their resources and I was leaving just before Christmas, at a time when healthcare needed nurses the most. But I was done and that was my timing. I was terrified to tell my manager that I was leaving after only being there less than a year, but I'm so glad that it got done.

From that day on I had to realize that I was not walking this journey alone. As easy as it is sometimes to try to collaborate with other people or share ideas or work together as a team, at the end of the day I have to know that the power lies within me. I have all the answers. I have internal guidance. I'm on my own unique path. Different people are attracted to me at different times, and I can trust all the energy that's in alignment now.

I led a retreat in a mansion in Thailand, something that had always been a dream of mine. Initially, when I booked this $10,000 villa with no funds in my account, I had planned to co-lead it with a friend of mine. One day as I was lying in the bathtub in Australia where I was living at the time, trying to fill up this retreat, I said to myself, "This isn't going to happen from anyone else except me. I can't co-lead this retreat because this is my dream, and I can't count on anyone to have the same vision that I have."

Four people came to that retreat. It was the most beautiful experience I ever had in my life. I became my higher self at that event. None of it would have happened if I hadn't gone after my dream and said yes and taken ownership of what was mine.

I think when it comes to these types of internal beliefs and patterns of not trusting ourselves, we need to learn that we're the ones with the power. Life has a way of leading us to learn that lesson more than one time.

Self-worth, especially for women, is probably the most necessary thing that anyone could teach. Women have so much wisdom and so many life experiences, and our brains work in a multi-focused fashion. We have the ability to completely transform lives with the emotionality and the love that we bring.

I know for myself that I was not taught how to be confident, how to stand up for myself, how to speak with elegance and grace, and set boundaries. I was not taught how to love and respect my body and appreciate all aspects of it. I was taught how to diet, I was taught how to moderate, and I was taught how to fix myself. I was taught that yelling was bad and emoting was not something anyone in my household wanted. I don't believe I had any sense of self. I don't believe that I had anyone reflecting back to me about life and whether the way I was acting worked with life or not. I remember feeling like an empty vessel, with not much or very little identity.

My journey in life has been to find out who she was. It's been the most magnificent journey. Women are creators. We constantly get to feel where we're at in our lives and make pivots as they come. We create based on what's going on in the present moment, and what that means is that there can also be major life shifts frequently or several times in life.

Each time I met with those familiar habits and patterns of asking other people and not trusting myself, feeling scared of all the logistics, and trying to analyze the entire situation. And time and time again what it always comes back down to is that connection that I have with source, with God, with my meditation, with my inner world, with making decisions based on what feels kind and loving and supportive to me.

I don't have to do it on my own, but I get to do it on my own. Because no one has the same path as I do. No one has the same life mission that I do, and neither do you. It's been nine years since I left my nursing job. Outside of working at a café two times a week while building my business, I have never had a formal job. In 2015 I became an entrepreneur, and I had absolutely no idea that what being an entrepreneur meant was being on a spiritual and personal development path for the rest of your life. It has been the most phenomenal journey of self-love, self-awareness, challenges, and life satisfaction.

One of my lifelong dreams was to travel around the world. I ended up taking my coaching business on the road. I worked and traveled in twelve countries for two and a half years. I went to the Taj Mahal in India, I went to Bali, I lived and backpacked in Australia, I backpacked the north and south islands of New Zealand, and I had some of the most extraordinary experiences. Everything on my bucket list was checked off—scuba diving in the Great Barrier Reef—just everything.

Today on two properties, one a house by a lake, I have a hot tub, a beautiful yard, and a beautiful, white Pomeranian dog. My life keeps getting better and better every day. I'm surrounded by beautiful women, friends, connections and colleagues. I have beautiful relationships with my family, I play pickleball twice a week, work out twice a week, and play kickball with friends—I have the most incredible clients and a fantastic team.

I'm a firm believer in the fact that anything is possible, and what I know is that alignment matters. If things start feeling hard and anxious and heavy, it's a sign that you may need to pivot and trust yourself again. Or maybe for the first time.

By the way, a sign that you're off track is the fact that your eating is off track—you're overeating, binging, and numbing with alcohol—these are the signs that you're off track. Start asking yourself the deeper questions. Start meditating, start listening; there's something that's being asked of you now, and it's not our analytical mind to try to figure it out. It's not just about meditating, it's about feeling into, about asking for guidance from someone who has experienced the same thing at times. But at the end of the day, making a big decision is not going to allow anyone else to make the leap except you. There is no skydiving instructor on your back.

You can do it. You can choose a life of spaciousness, of expansion, of peace, of inner freedom, and joy. You just need to choose it. You can choose a life of adventure and travel and fun—you can quite literally have it all. But at the end of the day, you're the only one who can make the decision and jump.

I learned with my leap of faith to leave my nursing job that God truly did have my back, and that I am the co-creator with God in my life.

Sometimes it doesn't make sense how we end up in toxic relationships, or why bad things happen to good people. But there are always actual answers as to why. None of us have to stay stuck. When you have the awareness of how your unconscious mind works and how patterning works and how emotions work, and pair up with someone who has gotten through the same and created something magnificent in their lives, you can again truly have anything. You can overcome anything. And I want that for you if you want that.

Absolutely knowing yourself, knowing your astrology, knowing your human design, knowing your family patterns, knowing your strengths—these tools have been accelerators to my alignment on my individual and unique path with pure confidence. Emotional mastery is a huge component. Joe Dispenza talks about how we can have the perfect diet, eat everything organic, be vegan, be vegetarian, be dairy-free, take the best supplements, have the best workout routines, but if we never learn how to respond to our environment and what's happening, our body continues to produce the hormones of stress that lead to cancer and disease. In my experience, my learning how to respond to my external world and respond to my inner world has been the most life-enhancing thing I've ever done. It's made me happier. It's made me healthier. And it's increased my faith in God.

John Maxwell has these principles for how to be successful, and I'll list them off: number one, reject rejection.; number two, vary your approach; number three, bounce back; number four, don't point fingers; number five, see failure as temporary; number six, set realistic expectations; and number seven, focus on strengths.

I love these principles. I love living a life of infinite possibility and creation. I'm grateful for all the teachers that have appeared exactly when I've been ready. I thank God for continuing to learn every day. And I will continue to share with others what I learned as I grow. I hope one day it can be instilled in my children, and until then, I'll keep working on a little child who continues to live inside me, waiting for me to continue to love and nurture and nourish her in ways not only I can say.

About The Author

Leslie Thornton

Leslie is the Founder and CEO of Hypnosis for Permanent Weight Loss, an international health coaching program for people seeking mental freedom from food, body, and weight, and is a leading expert in the holistic health space.

Connect with Leslie:

Chapter 10

Accepting Myself

by Jessica Herrera

HIGH SCHOOL IS A time of transformation for many of us whether we like it or not. My story is no different. Going into ninth grade, I had an amazing group of friends from church. We did nearly everything together, and I would say they were my ride or die besties. What people didn't know is that the group were not only my best friends but also my escape from the fighting and toxicity that I felt was always waiting for me at home.

About midway through high school, one of my friends had a birthday party that forever changed our lives. A massive argument broke out resulting in me feeling like I had to pick sides and ultimately, I lost my friends.

This happened at a particularly difficult time as I was also starting to have confusing thoughts about my sexuality. I grew up in the church and was taught that God hated homosexuals. By this time, one of my friends had already come out as a lesbian, and the church members were treating her and her partner poorly. They were not allowed to work with the kids at Bible camp, as if they would do something to harm a child because they liked each other. People in the congregation began to talk behind their backs and generally treated them like outcasts instead of continuing to show them love. As someone who was struggling with my own thoughts and feelings around my sexuality, I started to withdraw from the church.

At home, I was being called worthless and experiencing consistent hate and fighting. I woke up to being yelled at, which started each day off in a negative way and I began to hate myself. I hated that I had feelings for women, that God would hate me, and that my own family members had threatened to beat me up or disown me if I was gay. Eventually, the pain of losing my best friends, feeling worthless, unworthy of love, and knowing I was gay got to me. I went upstairs and grabbed the largest kitchen knife I could find before returning to the basement. I sat crying and writing in my journal, drawing a tombstone engraved "Jessica Hosler, 1988–2006." My face was burning as I screamed out to God, full of hate and anger toward my parents and myself. I remember calling out and asking why. As I held the knife to my stomach and tears streamed down my face, I rationalized why the world would be better off without me. I also felt fear and shame for even considering taking my life. I continued to release all my pent-up emotions until I didn't have any more hate or anger to give. I put down the knife and felt peace wash over me. *I chose life.*

This experience forced me to confront my emotions and choose to accept myself for who I really was. So what if I liked women more than men? My sexuality didn't make me a bad person, and anyone who felt that way didn't need to have a seat at my table. I no longer believed that God would hate me for simply loving someone who was not a man. I let love fill me up as I came to this realization and never looked back.

It took time and practice to become confident expressing who I am. I didn't need acceptance from others and truly claimed my power for the first time. Over the next year I began to embrace and accept myself, which was the most freeing feeling. I cut my hair as a sort of symbol to myself and declaration to the world that I don't give a fuck what they expected me to be. I became confident in my own way of being and attracted amazing opportunities for myself. I finished trade school with a 4.0 and received a job offer before graduation that led me to a six-figure income as a twenty-year-old. I felt on top of the world.

A Positive Shift

My life was on a positive trajectory for the next few years as I made friends in my new job and location. I had money, love, and a career that I was passionate about doing and sharing with others.

Unfortunately, what seemed like good fortune did not last forever as I started making decisions that did not serve me. I was a twenty-year-old who didn't know how to manage that kind of money and ended up with nothing to show for it. I made a triggered decision to leave my career with no real plan other than moving back home to Colorado and starting over. I quickly spent any savings I had once I got to Colorado and bounced around for a few years trying to get my feet back under me. Having no plan and no vision of what I really wanted was unknowingly keeping me stuck.

By 2013, I regained some traction with a job that made me feel financially secure again. I was not even close to my past income, but I was able to provide for my needs and finally have fun again when I wanted. Then it felt like the rug was pulled out from under me as I was laid off. I had recently purchased a new car and signed a lease with a roommate but had not rebuilt my savings. Unemployment barely covered my rent. It did not take long before I had no money and was unsure where I would get my next tank of gas or groceries from.

This time, I turned to God, not to yell and scream but for comfort. I started listening to K-LOVE radio all the time and found that I was able to handle the situation in a positive manner. I am not saying I was not stressed as I missed car payments and contemplated the possibility of needing to move in with my mom or become homeless, but I never gave up.

It was not lost on me that the music I listened to had a major impact on my mood and ability to handle the stress happening in my life. I became thankful for the things I still had instead of angry about the things I didn't. I was thankful for my beautiful friend Kyssandra who took me out to a Valentine's lunch knowing I wouldn't have been able to otherwise. I became thankful that I had unemployment to cover rent and my roommate who helped me with utilities during that time. I was thankful I had a mom to run home to if things got worse.

At this point, I became a believer in the power of positive thought as my life began to pick back up again. Someone took a chance on me and hired me for a job that I had *no idea* what I was getting into. That chance paid off, as I quickly made a name for myself and learned the instrumentation they hired me to work on. This job had all the things I was missing since my first career job. I was financially stable, building my credit back up, traveling, and enjoying the work again. This time around, nobody understood what I did, but it didn't matter because I loved the work and felt challenged.

Layoffs struck again, and while painful to experience, this time I was prepared with the tools to manage the situation. The management from that company reached out to my current company and gave me an amazing heartfelt recommendation. Their efforts on my behalf set the wheels in motion for my life to take off in a way that was better than I could have ever imagined.

Owning my power in a positive mindset is one hundred percent the reason I ended up in my current company. It is funny how things in life that feel tragic can lay the foundation for an amazing future. You must be open-minded enough to see it for something other than a negative experience. As I reflect on my life, every big moment that felt like a gut punch was paving the way for a better plan than I could have imagined.

During that transition period between jobs, I had also started dating again. My positive mindset allowed me to show up as my authentic self for her, despite the challenges I was facing. A year later, I proposed to my beautiful girlfriend, we bought a house, and started a journey remodeling it together. I taught myself how to do everything from framing to electrical work to plumbing and drywall as we finished our basement and created a home. All through the power of a positive mindset and belief in myself.

A few years later, we got married and began the journey of trying to become parents. Without a positive outlook, I can say that my wife and I would have given up, as our journey was not an easy one. Over three years we did six IUIs and, ultimately, five transfer cycles of IVF. In that experience, we were on a roller coaster of emotions, as we would get excited about the possibility of being pregnant and then a short depression as we kept getting a no. In 2021, we had finally gotten a strong positive test and knew we were going to have a baby girl. One of the ultrasound appointments didn't look good, as the heart rate was not as fast as the medical team wanted it to be. We anxiously waited for the next appointment to find we lost our little girl to a miscarriage. This was the most painful moment of my life.

My wife and I both had to process our emotions and reach closure in our own way and time. Remaining in my power and having faith we would be successful, we continued to try. Two transfer cycles later, we were blessed to be pregnant with a little boy who is now five months old at the time I am writing this.

I believe being in your power looks different for everyone and in that experience, my power was being resilient, positive, and supportive of the process we were going through. You can probably see how easy it would be to look at any of those negative experiences from high school to now and become defeated or adopt a victim mentality. The reality is, our baby boy came at the perfect time for us and is the most perfect representation of joy.

Claiming My Power

As a new parent, I have the desire to be the best version of myself for my son so he can be the best version of himself. Before his birth, I had become complacent in my health and gained weight over the relationship and especially during my wife's pregnancy. There is no chance I am going to be a parent that doesn't play with my child outside, or who cannot keep up. This means I had to approach my health differently and started to make changes early on in 2023.

It has been my year for transformation in so many ways. Starting with my health, I saw an ad for a program that I felt drawn to and joined. To my surprise, this program was unlike any other I had experienced. They addressed a lot of the mental hurdles that people experience on a weight loss journey and had several guest speakers. This is how I was introduced to Elyse Archer.

My earliest conversation with Elyse challenged what I wanted. I searched long and hard for what exactly I wanted out of life as I created my vision. What am I living for? What would make me feel complete when I pass on? The answer for me was family. I am committed to being loving, available, and supportive to my family. I wanted to be able to give back to the world and make a difference. From there, it seems like the building blocks of this chapter in life started to assemble themselves for me.

Not long after, I reached out to Sarit (one of the founders of the fitness program I am in) and inquired about working with her. She asked probing questions, as the amazing leader she is, and found I wanted to improve my communication skills as they impact all areas of my life. That is when she showed up as an angel and recommended a particular leadership program. I trusted her and signed up right away.

Amazingly enough, this training was in complete alignment with Elyse's coachings, and I created a fast track to becoming a person who will change the world. I was able to let go of the one-sided perspective that I was holding on to about how things have happened for me in life. I no longer felt pain or anger toward my parents, and most importantly, I found the ability to feel worthy of love and abundance. How many of us walk around feeling like we must earn love? I have a feeling a lot of us do. I am here to tell you that once you learn to love yourself and know that you are worthy, you will unlock a freedom you could not have imagined.

I have stepped into my power, my elevated self, and I can physically and emotionally feel the difference. When my higher self is in control, I stand taller, am full of confidence, feel lighter, and I don't walk around in this space of anxiety and fear like I used to. I own that I am a powerful, passionate, authentic leader with every fiber of my being. That may sound a bit weird for people to hear; it feels a bit weird to say, honestly.

It is important to understand that claiming your power is not a one-time event. You don't go to training, feel powerful, and never falter again. In the words of a friend of mine, it is like learning to ride a bike. When you first claim your power, it is like hopping on the bike for the first time. You make a conscious decision to overcome your fear of failure, being humiliated, looking silly, or potentially getting hurt. Then you still have to learn as you go. You will lose balance sometimes, giving in to the gremlins that kept you from riding in the first place. The more you practice, the easier it becomes. Your increased awareness of the gremlins allows you to be in your power more often and have a smoother ride. You may even get so distracted you forget to look where you are going and hit a parked car. I am pretty sure that is a rite of passage anyway. Before you know it, your higher self is fully in control, and you have the confidence to ride with no hands.

What phase are you in? Maybe you haven't been able to claim your power yet and are on the sidelines, afraid like I was last year. Or maybe you are wobbling along and practicing like I currently am.

I recently learned that Michelangelo used a discarded and rejected piece of marble for his famous statue *David*. Others had attempted to create something with the piece and then gave up due to its poor quality and the seemingly impossible feat. It then sat and degraded for a quarter century before Michelangelo took on the project, taking three years to complete. He said all he had to do was chip away all of the parts that weren't *David* to reveal him.

Similarly, we can continue to chip away at the things that are not our higher self and do not serve us—like guarded hearts, distraction, hatred, and anger. It doesn't matter how broken or unworthy we feel now, it doesn't matter what we have done to others or what they have done to us; we are all beautiful beings capable of being a *David*. It isn't always easy and is a lifelong commitment of exploration, improvement, and acceptance to become a *David* or unleash our higher self. However, we are worth it and we can all choose life. There is risk involved as you become more vulnerable, loving, joyful, and connected in this life, but the cost of not doing it is far greater than any risk.

What would you find in yourself as you claim your power and continue to progress? What is hiding under the marble that others discard? What are you willing to risk by letting your higher self take control and be visible?

I know I can change the world by supporting millions of leaders in creating connected, joyful, passionate places to work. I can help them avoid the costly mistakes we make as new leaders and navigate tough situations. I know I can make a difference in this world as my higher self. Now that I have claimed my power, I know this. I am committed to creating a world of love, authenticity, connection, joy, and commitment. I will do this by living as if it has already happened. What will you do?

About The Author

Jessica Herrera

Jessica Herrera is a widely regarded leadership coach for emerging female leaders in male-dominated industries.

With a degree in Business Administration with a concentration in Organizational Leadership, and over 14 years of experience in industries like aviation and scientific instrumentation, Jessica is a passionate and authentic leader who is committed to developing others and creating fun and rewarding workplaces for everyone she works with.

A leader in her field and part of the LGBTQ+ community, Jessica knows that being able to lead others powerfully starts with personal leadership, self-acceptance, and love.

As a coach and mentor, Jessica is available to help emerging leaders gain the confidence and skills they need to achieve their goals and live out their biggest impact.

Connect with Jessica:

Chapter 11

It's All Part of the Journey

by Christina Vieira

I DON'T BELIEVE THERE is any one moment where you give yourself permission and everything changes. I believe there's a series of choices where you decide to step into your power. And just like everything else, it is a muscle and it needs to be exercised.

I will speak to the one moment where I made this realization. I was sitting on the couch after my third failed IVF transfer, watching *Yellowstone*, eating sushi, drinking wine, and sobbing. This transfer may have been just one more disappointment added to years of fertility treatments.

But this one felt different. It felt like a loss. It felt like a dream I had about a big family and kids running in and out of a busy kitchen, grabbing lemonade and snacks off the counter on their way through was starting to fade. It was the first time in three years of fertility treatments that I allowed myself to grieve.

I allowed myself to feel the loss of every plan I had made for my family.

It was also the first time I gave myself permission to fail.

I am the oldest of four children and the only girl. I was destined by birth order to achieve. I was told at a young age that getting good grades and a scholarship to college was my job. And I accomplished it and everything else I set my mind to. (Except for starring in the school musical and going on to Broadway because my singing voice did not get the memo.)

But like most overachievers, I was dealing with a lot of anxiety.

I was a people pleaser who would become whoever I thought I needed to be to be liked in whatever group I was currently with.

I resisted acknowledging the symptoms because I had a great childhood. I had everything I needed. I didn't have the alcoholic father and narcissistic mother that someone very close to me was trying to heal. But the only coping mechanism I had was shopping. Online of course. The thought of going into a store where I didn't know where things were and where other people might see and judge me put me into a full-blown panic attack. But instead of dealing with my anxiety, I would buy things for a dopamine hit to make myself feel better.

I would buy things to encapsulate the person I thought the people at work, my friends, or my family wanted me to be. I would buy things for other people hoping they would give me the love I wasn't giving myself. When I had maxed out the credit cards and hid yet another purchase, I almost lost my marriage.

So the time I ever gave myself permission to be powerful was about ten years ago when I first started seeing a therapist. I have heard so many stories of people going to one or two sessions and when they are not cured, think therapy didn't work. This, like anything else, is a process and a journey. My first therapist was very sweet but was mostly just a person to talk to. You have to keep trying until you find the right person for you.

It wasn't long after that I was laid off from my job planning events at a tech company, and I began the journey of an entrepreneur. Fortunately, I had started planning Disney vacations as a side hustle about a year before I lost my job. The plan was to build my business to the point where it replaced my full-time income in three to five years. But with massive debt and no salary coming in, I gave myself permission to pursue my passion. I loved helping families get away from the day-to-day hustle and bustle and spend time reconnecting.

One thing I will say about the travel industry when I entered it in 2016 is that it was cutthroat and very negative. Everyone seemed to have a scarcity mindset. No one wanted to help each other out or share best practices. When you would ask an established agent where they got their clients, they would answer, "Repeat guests and referrals." Okay, so where did you get your clients who became repeat guests?" I actually had someone say to me, "I had to work hard to figure it out. You should too."

But I loved my clients. I particularly enjoyed helping moms allow someone to help with the vacation planning and to actually enjoy their vacation as well. In 2018, after over a year of trying, six months of tests and insurance paperwork, and one round of fertility medications, I became a mom myself. When my baby girl looked up at me with her dad's gorgeous eyelashes, I knew I needed to do something different. I needed to create a space where community was more important than competition. Where women supported women.

I gave myself permission to change the industry. I left my agency in 2019 and started Showcase the World Travel in November. There is nothing more you can do for your self-awareness than starting a company. Despite just getting out of the clutches of debt, I entered it again, this time to build a website, develop a brand, and—the best money I have ever spent—hire a business coach.

That was the best permission I gave myself. To ask for help. I had never built a business before. I was expecting her to share marketing tactics and help me manage the books. But she did so much more. She introduced me to the idea of meditation and the law of attraction. She helped me develop a morning routine that put me first, even though I had a six-month-old. She even inspired me to find a therapist who was a better fit. To teach me the skills to love myself. To start figuring out who I was after a decade of being who I thought others wanted me to be.

I set out to create a travel agency that was collaborative, a team that shared best practices and proposal templates. I used my knowledge of sales training to create a curriculum that went beyond how to make a booking to how to build a business.

Which brings me to my next dramatic moment of permission. I started a travel business in November 2019. You may not know but travel advisers make a majority of their income from commissions on the packages they sell. They receive the commission after a client has booked. So when I started my agency in late 2019, most of the trips I was booking were for 2020.

The summer of 2020 was the darkest of my life. My husband manages a town and, therefore, is responsible for all the essential workers. He was working nonstop and spent many nights sleeping on the floor in his office. I was home alone with an eighteen-month-old and a failing business. I was working so hard to cancel trips, get refunds, and reschedule. I spent hour upon hour upon hour rescheduling trips—never seeing a cent. I felt so alone, I felt so unseen. I started to question everything. Was I going to put my family into financial jeopardy again to continue following a dream I didn't know was even possible?

When I started the business, I certainly did not expect to be profitable in my first year; I was hoping to break even with a little profit coming in around year two. I did not expect the entire industry to shut down for over a year and for consumers to not be comfortable traveling for another year after that. Every time there would be a glimmer of hope, a new variant would mean another round of cancellations.

October 2020 was set to be the month everything changed. The month the business could support itself without draining our personal accounts. It was the most bookings I ever had in a month, and I felt it was going to finally change everything. Then Delta hit and every single one of those bookings canceled.

That was the moment I almost gave up.

I spent a week looking at all the money and time I put into my company. What my losses would be if I simply walked away. That was the moment I gave myself permission to not give up, because I saw the potential in the business. I saw my daughter taking over for me when I am ready to retire. I doubled down. I invested in technology, I doubled my Facebook ad spending, I hired an assistant.

As hard as this period of time was, it wasn't just hard for me. It was hard for everyone in the travel space. For everyone in the world really. But what it did for travel was astounding. People started coming together, they started supporting each other. The "old guard" who liked doing things the way they always did decided to not continue beyond the pandemic. There were major changes coming to the industry, and I knew I had something to add.

I gave myself permission to share my knowledge. I partnered with a friend to start a business to support travel advisers in building systems in their businesses. The company took off immediately. We had found a need that no one else realized. We made six figures in our first year and won industry awards. The year 2022 was a great year for me professionally. The agency was finally able to support itself. I started bringing on agents. I was in such a great headspace and finally felt my value...as long as I was in motion and accomplishing things in business.

My personal life on the other hand was a mess. I could not separate myself from my work. If I lost a client or didn't have a great month, I went into a spiral of self-doubt. I was easily triggered by my husband and daughter. I was constantly exhausted. We started fertility treatments again in early 2021. Remember, I had a dream of a large family. I saw us all traveling together for two weeks every June when they were out of school. Scavenger hunts in the Louvre, eating gelato in Italy, African safaris for high school graduation. I have a bond with my brothers that I desperately wanted for my daughter.

So we started living our lives in six-week cycles. We never knew when I would need to be home for an ultrasound, trigger shot, or transfer. Now, being a planner my entire life, not knowing if I could go on that trip in two months, was torture. Not to mention all of the hormones being pumped into my body and not feeling like my body is my own. Each and every cycle was a disappointment that needed to be grieved. But I needed to stay in motion. I needed to not think about how I was feeling and just push it down and push through. If it is not this one, it will be the next one. We will move that trip to California to next month.

Everything was in turmoil, but I would not acknowledge it.

This past January, I went to Sedona with Elyse. She was going to help me expand both my businesses. But sitting in a room with a dozen women I didn't know, she helped me give myself permission to feel. To feel the sorrow, the grief—not just for the baby I didn't have but for the plans that I had made.

I had my next transfer the following week and truly believed because I had processed so much, this was going to be the one that worked. It didn't. Which brings me back to the sushi, wine, and sobbing on the couch. I gave myself permission to fail. I gave myself permission to not continue IVF. I gave myself permission to take my body back.

I am still completely open to adding another soul to our family. I have plenty of love to give. But I wasn't the best mom I could possibly be to the incredible, extremely funny, exceptionally smart, and soulful girl I already have. I knew the last three years was a lesson in letting go. To not holding on to plans so tightly. To being flexible and accepting failure, despite being so goal-driven. It was in that moment that I realized it is all a part of my journey.

I may not hit every business goal I set for myself, but I will make progress toward them. I may not become my best self overnight, but every day I become stronger and love myself a little more. So you see, for me, it is a series of moments. They build on each other. While you may give yourself permission in one area of your life, you may be withholding it in another. It is a trust that everything is happening for me. Any decision I make is the highest and best because it is either getting me closer to where I want to be or teaching me a lesson I need to learn to get there. I don't know what I will need to give myself permission to do next, but I can't wait to see what it will be.

About The Author

Christina Vieira

Christina Vieira is the founder of Showcase the World Travel, a modern travel agency for overwhelmed families. She has planned hundreds of trips for parents of young children who need a break from the busy. With a degree in Events Management from Suffolk University and 6 years planning marketing events and managing sales team travel she has always loved handling all the often-forgotten details.

She is widely regarded in the Travel Industry for her unique planning processes and use of modern technology. This led her to co-found Magic Made Simple, a media company that encourages travel entrepreneurs to uplevel their businesses with workflows and systems, with Penelope Cooper.

She is a member of the Family Travel Association, American Society of Travel Advisors, Travel Weekly Magellan Award Winner, and was honored as a Future Leader in Travel. Her insights have been featured on podcasts like Vacation Mavens, Travelling Entrepreneur, and Wicked Good Moms, and is a recurring guest on WJXT Channel 4 Morning Show in Jacksonville Florida.

She believes vacation is where families really thrive, kids grow to love learning, and our best memories are made and loves that she is able to help busy Moms who don't have time to plan it all finally take a vacation they don't have to worry about and the whole family can enjoy, for a change.

Connect with Christina: